Students Speak

Effective Discipline for Today's Students

Building a Sense of Community

By Linda Clarry Barber & Betsy Geddes, Ed.D.

Published by Brandon Publishing Co.
Portland, Oregon 97282 USA

ISBN 0-09664800-C-7

*To everyone who
has ever taught a child.*

TABLE OF CONTENTS

STUDENTS SPEAK: EFFECTIVE DISCIPLINE FOR TODAY'S STUDENTS

THE STORY BEHIND STUDENTS SPEAK

It all began when the authors met while working together in a Portland, Oregon school. Betsy had been assigned there as a principal, and Linda had been a teacher and team leader there for many years. The school had lots of problems. The kids were out of control and running amok. Test scores had fallen. Morale was at an all-time low. It wasn't that the teachers weren't working hard, it was just that the teachers were doing all the work and the students were taking responsibility for nothing. Our task was to pull the place together.

That first year there were good times and bad. Using the traditional techniques of reward and punishment, we did get order in the school. However, test scores did not go up, and nobody was happy. In fact, we got in trouble at the end of the year because our suspension rate was the highest in the city and our budgets were depleted. It was becoming apparent that the traditional tools of reward and punishment were not bringing about the desired results. Teachers were still unhappy, kids were still apathetic or running amok, and test scores were going no place.

That summer we went looking for a better way: a way to teach students to take responsibility for their learning and behavior, while bringing the joy of teaching back to the staff. What we found and what we subsequently implemented is what we are presenting to you in this book.

Looking back on those years the answer was really always right in front of our eyes. We discovered that in order to bring about behavioral change and increase academic learning all we had to do was look to the kids. Once we understood what their basic needs were, and figured out how to help them fulfill those needs, life got better for everybody. We don't want you to spend years searching like we did, so we have written this book to share our discoveries with you.

WHAT THIS BOOK CAN DO FOR YOU

This book will help you rediscover the joy of teaching and empower you to teach kids how to take responsibility for their behavior and their learning. You will accomplish this by learning from the first half of this book what basic interaction needs students are looking to have fulfilled when they come to your classroom. The second half of this book will provide you with stimulating yet practical lesson plans that you can use in your classroom to help students fulfill the needs. **Students whose needs are addressed tend to take responsibility for their behavior and learning. Kids whose needs are not addressed, don't.**

WHAT ARE KIDS' BASIC NEEDS?

When kids come together in the school setting, they have the following four needs: the need for **INCLUSION**, to be "in"; the need for **CONTROL**, to have some say in what happens; the need for **AFFECTION**, to like and be liked; and the need for **COMPETENCY**, to be seen as capable. **To the extent we can help kids fulfill these needs, we bond them to us, to the school, and to an ongoing love of education. When the needs aren't fulfilled in kids, they are driven from us.**

THE PITHY POINT

The way to get kids to be responsible, own and solve their problems, do their work, and behave in a somewhat reasonable manner is to address their basic needs.

HOW DO WE KNOW IF KIDS' NEEDS ARE BEING FULFILLED?

The best way is to ask kids and examine our own behavior. We have developed several surveys to be used to do just this. These surveys will help you understand to what extend students believe their needs are being fulfilled in the classroom. They will also help you examine your own behavior in relation to need fulfillment.

HOW DO WE HELP THEM FULFILL THEIR NEEDS?

I GOT IT!

Being responsible is a learned behavior and must be taught. I guess I'll have to teach it.

The answer lies in **WINNING WAYS**. **WINNING WAYS** are (1) techniques for changing your behavior, (2) skills to teach kids to use to change their behavior, and (3) classroom activities that develop and reinforce the four basic needs. We have designed them specifically for use with students of all ages and abilities, and in any school setting.

CHAPTER 1
OUR CHANGING WORLD

IN THIS CHAPTER

- ⊚ Why is punishment not working?

- ⊚ What ever happened to bribing them with rewards?

- ⊚ Just what is discipline anyway?

- ⊚ What kind of discipline works today?

Chapter 1

OUR CHANGING WORLD

On the surface, kids today seem so different than we were at their age. They must face the usual problems of growing up, as well as the more complex problems that our society poses today. With more parents working longer hours, kids often have less guidance than in years past, and may lack the personal discipline to deal adequately with the demands placed on them.

PUNISHMENT AND REWARD

How would you react to this situation? A fifth grade teacher shoves a boy from her P.E. class into the office and says, "Do something with him. I'm not getting paid enough to listen to this stuff." The boy had been acting up in gym, and when asked to take some time out on the bench, he had turned on the teacher and called her the "B" word (which as you know, does not mean "beautiful teacher").

How might we discipline this student? Based on the old methods with which we were raised and trained to handle kids in school, we would probably use one of two approaches: punishment or reward. We could punish the student for using the "B" word, or reward him for promising never to use the word again. But neither of these approaches will bring about the desired results in today's classrooms. The results we are looking for are first, **an internalized change in the student's behavior, sustained over a period of time,** and second, and of equal importance, **is for us as educators to rediscover the joy of teaching.**

Why don't we get the same compliance from the punishment and reward systems that our parents and teachers got from us? The answer can be very complicated, but rather than lay blame on the kids, we must recognize this cultural and environmental fact: the world has changed. Our parents and teachers got compliance from us because we feared their punishments, and we wanted their rewards. "Please don't tell my parents," we begged when getting in trouble, the prospect of punishment certain. And any little reward handed out by the school staff was a memorable occasion to be treasured forever.

Today most students neither fear what we can do to them nor really want what we can give them. In other words, punishment and rewards have lost their effectiveness. Thanks to the way schools are regulated now, we cannot inflict enough pain, or lavish enough rewards on students to get them to shape up. The last time one of the authors told a student that he would be welcome to eat in the school cafeteria only after cleaning up the mess he'd made or paying back the custodian for his time and effort, a lawyer appeared the next day, saying that the student's rights had been violated and demanding that the student be fed immediately. And, how many teachers today have enough money in their personal checking accounts or school budgets to buy the kids off on a regular basis? A few M&M's in kindergarten might work well, but by high school most kids think a little red Porsche would be much move motivating.

As the old cliché goes, "There is good news and there is bad news." First let's look at the reasons why the old models of punishment and reward are just not effective with today's students. Then we'll explore the less familiar techniques that are proving more effective.

THE PITHY POINT
Punishment and rewards, the techniques we learned from our teachers and our parents, are not effective with today's kids.

LOOKING AT WHY PUNISHMENT IS INEFFECTIVE

Looking back at the kid who called his teacher the "B" word, that teacher might say, "Don't you ever, ever use that word in my room, do you hear me? Now, you write fifty times, I will never call my teacher a b—— again." Or the student might be sent from the room to be disciplined by a higher authority: "Take this referral to the principal, and don't come back till you learn never to say that word again!" And then the principal might say, "You're suspended for three days, and don't let me ever hear you say that word in this school again!"

To most of us, this punitive approach sounds familiar because that's the way school was for us. And our teachers did get what they wanted from us: compliance. Many of us learned from punishment what **not** to do. Unfortunately, we did not learn what **to do**. The nun's story illustrates this point.

THE NUN FROM HELL

When Linda was in first grade at Our Lady of Perpetual Terror, she had a teacher who was "the nun from hell." This nun paraded around the room in her long, flowing robes, ruler in hand, slapping anyone's hands who happened to be doing something she thought inappropriate. Unfortunately, Linda was one of the "talkers" in the class, so she went home with bloody knuckles on a regular basis. Linda hated the nun's cruelty and feared what she believed to be the nun's "supernatural powers."

Linda's recesses were spent trying to enlist other kids to mutiny. Not once did she think, "If I would be quiet during class, I wouldn't get smacked." Needless to say, Linda didn't learn much that year. Instead, she focused on her anger toward the nun. If the teacher had just said, "Linda, could you help me out and refrain from talking when I am?" or "I teach best when others are quiet." she would have neutralized the bad feeling, identified the problem, and focused Linda's attention on the specific issue. Unfortunately she chose punishment, which led Linda to blame the nun rather than her own disruptive behavior.

WHAT'S THE POINT?

Choose a positive over a negative. Most of us have been taught that the way to discipline students who make inappropriate choices is to respond negatively. A more effective approach is to provide the students with the guidance they need to recognize, own up to, and solve the problem themselves. This lets students know that we believe them to be capable of making good decisions. This method of dealing with disruption frees teachers from blame and makes us feel more in control. In reality, we are sharing the control.

LOOKING AT WHY REWARDS DON'T WORK

Contrary to the way our generation was raised, we rarely will get sustained, internalized behavior change with today's students by using rewards. A typical reward response to the above swearing problem would be to approach the student with, "You know we don't use that kind of language in our school. I have a card here with ten squares, which I will staple in your folder. For every day that you don't say that word, I'll put a check mark in one of the squares. When you have 10 checks, you can have a free period. Now doesn't that sound wonderful?"

Whereas weak rewards rarely work at all, even good rewards can be ineffective. The following story illustrates this point.

THE CLASSROOM WITH EVERYTHING

Mrs. Jones was a third grade teacher. She spent hours planning lessons. She included everything a principal or parent could want in her curriculum, teaching to various learning styles and making her classroom beautiful and interesting. She also devised a reward system that included ways for students to earn rewards as individuals, as a part of a group, and as a whole class.

As time went on, Mrs. Jones was forced to add more and more rules when students discovered loopholes to get around specific areas. She also had to spend more time inventing or creating the rewards, so that the students wouldn't get bored. Issuing rewards took a lot of class time, and the record keeping became tedious. The kids began to demand rewards for everything they did. If they did their homework, they wanted a reward. If they watered the plants, they wanted another.

Groups began to fight among themselves about how to handle their projects, and soon only the top academic students in each group were doing the work, while the average and struggling students caused mayhem in the classroom. The whole-class reward system led to peer pressure against those who chose not to participate fully. Soon the class's unity began to unravel.

Mrs. Jones's class was coming apart. She couldn't understand why because she thought she was

4

rewarding each and every student's accomplishment. She was now spending more time on class-room management than on curriculum. Her reward system had malfunctioned.

WHAT'S THE POINT?

Rewards and recognition are separate. They do not mean the same thing. Rewards tend to pander to the not-so-nice part of people. They set us apart, and soon we begin to expect rewards for things that we do on a regular basis. When group or whole-class rewards are dependent on individual behaviors, they can undermine and destroy class unity, building un-healthy competition and leading to diminished self-esteem for certain students.

Recognition, on the other hand, can upgrade self-esteem and develop higher goal-setting. Rec-ognition of achievement is important to all of us. It feels good to be acknowledged for some-thing outstanding or unusual we have done. But while recognition has its place, we want students to develop the understanding that much of what we do in life is for our own enrich-ment, whether others acknowledge it or not.

DISCIPLINE FOR CHANGING TIMES

Changing times call for changing ideas about discipline. Let's go back to the student who lost his temper in gym and called his teacher the "B" word. Today's teachers need a variety of skills to use when things go wrong. The skill selected depends on the teacher, the student, the relation-ship between the two, how many times the act has occurred, as well as school and community expectations and other variables. A teacher might say, "I need you to wait in the hall. I'll be out to discuss this with you in a moment." Or, "Take this referral and go to the office. You and I will talk later." Or even, "Is this the way we speak in this school? Yes or no? Do you think you and I can work it out, or do you think we need to get your parents involved?" No matter the approach, the purpose will be to eventually get the student to admit to and to solve the problem she has just created for herself.

Returning once again to the student who used the "B" word, let's look at how the principal handled the situation using the problem solving approach. "You see," the principal said, "I did not call your teacher the "B" word, you did. You must have been pretty angry to do that. Now, how are you going to get her to take you back? Do you think just saying you're sorry will do, or do you think you will have to offer to do more to make amends? Do you think bursting into the classroom to talk to her while she is teaching will work? Or do you think making an appoint-ment might work better? Please describe to me in detail your plan for handling this problem." After the student had done so, the principal added, "By the way, feel free to return to class when this matter is settled. Thanks."

What we are doing here is changing the definition of discipline. The old definition of discipline taught to us by our teachers and parents focused on getting compliance through the use of reward and punishment. Today's definition of discipline refers to its Latin root, *discipulus,* from which also comes the word disciple, meaning to *walk in the footsteps of my leader.* In other words, are we modeling and teaching on a daily basis the behavior we want to see in our children?

I GOT IT!
I can't change the behavior of the kids, so I'll have to work on changing mine.

In order for a child's behavior to change, we must model and teach the behaviors we want to see. If we are not modeling and teaching these behaviors, then it is our behavior that needs to change.

CHAPTER 2
STUDENTS' FOUR BASIC NEEDS

IN THIS CHAPTER

- ⚅ What are the four basic needs?

- ⚅ Do all students have them?

- ⚅ What happens if these needs aren't met?

- ⚅ Is it possible to meet these needs in today's schools?

Chapter 2

STUDENTS' FOUR BASIC NEEDS

When a baby is born it has five physical needs; eye contact, touch, smile, movement, and something warm to drink. If any of these needs are not fulfilled, the baby may fail to thrive or die. In a few short years the baby begins to interact with others; family, playmates, and kids at school. Now the child is faced with another set of needs; inclusion, control, affection, and competency. These are the basic interaction needs that all human beings have when two or more people come together. Just as with the physical needs, if any of these interaction needs are not fulfilled, the child, while not actually dying, may wither inside and fail to thrive. To the extent that we in school can help students fulfill these four basic interaction needs, we will bond them to us, to the school, and to a lifelong love of learning. To the extent that we don't address these needs, we will drive our children from us and from society as a whole.

LOOKING AT THE FOUR BASIC NEEDS

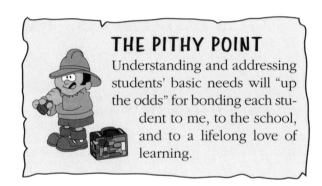

THE PITHY POINT
Understanding and addressing students' basic needs will "up the odds" for bonding each student to me, to the school, and to a lifelong love of learning.

When two or more people come together, as in the family or in the school setting, they come looking to fulfill four basic needs. The first is the need for **INCLUSION**, to be "in" or part of the "in" group. The second is the need for **CONTROL**, to be able to make decisions in their daily lives. The third need is the need for **AFFECTION**, to know there are people they can like, and who like them. The fourth need is the need for **COMPETENCY**, the need to be seen as capable in their daily lives and in the school setting. Taken together these needs form what is called a sense of belonging, a sense of family, or as some say, a sense of community.

All people, except perhaps for the severely emotionally disturbed or for those who have attained great maturity, enter the group setting looking to fulfill these needs, generally in the order listed above. When these needs are fulfilled, the person bonds with the group. When these needs are not fulfilled one of two things begins to happen. First, the behavior begins to go in one of two directions. If the person tends toward aggression, he or she will begin to act out. If the person has a more passive personality, he or she will begin to withdraw. Second, if the person cannot find a sense of family or belonging in the setting they are in, they will do whatever it takes to find that feeling in another setting.

In each person the needs have varying importance. For example, some of us have a high need for inclusion while in others this need is much lower. The importance of the needs can vary from situation to situation. Affection may be of higher importance to some in the family setting than in their work place. In short, this subject can be quite complicated. For the purpose of this book, we are going to keep it simple. And though we keep it simple, we will demonstrate how an understanding of this concept can be extremely helpful as we work to engage our students in behaving and learning.

HOW BEHAVIOR SLIDES WHEN THE NEEDS AREN'T MET

INCLUSION is the first need. It is the need to be "in," specifically to be "in" with what is considered to be the "in" group. In the school setting the main criteria for fulfilling this need is to have the right clothes or "the look." If you are a girl, it helps to be pretty, perky, and thin. If you are a boy, it helps to be macho, masculine, and athletic. So kids come to school, look around, and quickly decide whether they are "in" or "out." If they feel "in" they tend to settle down and attend to the assigned task. These are the kids we find easy to teach because they cause us relatively few problems. It's the kids who don't feel "in" who turn our hair gray and disrupt the learning process. The aggressive kids whose need for inclusion is not fulfilled will begin to act out, doing things like blurting out, calling attention to themselves, dressing in weird ways, throwing things, or making fun of others. In general, they keep the class in an uproar, focusing attention on themselves. The kids with more passive personalities will begin to withdraw. They will sit quietly, won't interact with others or participate in class, avoid eye contact, and if possible, try to physically escape the school setting.

Starting with the first day of class our role is to provide activities so that all kids in the class interact with each other on a regular basis. It is not enough for us to get to know the kids and the kids to get to know us. It is essential that each student gets to know every other student. Our own behavior and the activities we provide need to send the message that every kid in this classroom is "in."

THE PITHY POINT
Everybody needs to get to know everybody.

CONTROL is the second need. It is the need students have to have some, but not too much control in their lives. Students start testing us on the very first day of school to see how much control they can have. They hop up and down, they sharpen their pencil when we are talking, they ask what time lunch will be, they say "I have to go to the bathroom now." If the student has been in the school for any time at all, or has older brothers and sisters, they already know the answers to these questions. They are simply testing for teacher reaction, or degree of control. If the kids find they have some, but not too much control, they will settle down and attend to the task at hand. It's when kids find out they will have no control in the classroom, (when the teacher tells them everything to do and when and how to do it), or when the classroom is so loose that the kids have total control of the classroom and of the teacher, that things get ugly. The aggressive kids will take control in a ways that teachers know they are being had. The more passive kids will also take control, but so subtly teachers won't even know what's hit them. Kids learn that they can control the color of our faces, the tone of our voices, whether we teach the lesson or not, whether the assembly goes well, or the field trip is a nightmare, and whether the bathrooms are trashed and there is graffiti all over the building. In today's society they have even learned that they can control what happens to our teaching careers. There is not a kid in this country who does not understand that if they really want to take control of our lives all they have to do is go tell someone that we looked at them "funny," talked to them inappropriately, or touched them in a private place, and they can make our lives a living hell.

THE PITHY POINT
Teachers and students who share the control, work in greater harmony.

Providing kids with an appropriate amount of control is a very difficult task. Too much or too little and the situation quickly gets out of hand. However it is essential in both the behavioral and academic areas to provide opportunities for kids to make decisions about what happens. Our role as teachers is to give kids enough control to satisfy their need, while at the same time maintaining the control we need to effectively teach the class.

AFFECTION is the third need. It is the need to love and be loved, or like and be liked if love is too strong a term. Students, after figuring out where they stand on inclusion and just how much control they're going to have, begin to look around to see who they can like and who's going to like them. If they form friendships with other kids, and find teachers they like and who seem to care about them, they begin to relax and attend to the task at hand. If they aren't able to form friendships, and they believe their teachers hate them, then as with inclusion and control, their behavior will begin to slide in one of two directions. Aggressive kids will act out, wanting to be the center of attention, often taking the role of class clown or class bully. Those with more passive personalities will begin to withdraw, sitting quietly, avoiding eye contact, making no effort to form friendships or participate in any classroom or school activities. They can become like the student in "The Cipher in the Snow," who was such a total nonentity that when he stepped off the school bus and died in the snow, no one could recall anything about him or even remember him being in school.

Real teaching involves working with the whole child, meaning presenting the curriculum and building the relationship. Teaching the curriculum is generally easier to understand; building the relationship is a little more difficult. Our role is to provide activities and model behavior that sends the message that we all like each other. To put it bluntly, it is essential that students know that even if they lose their temper on Monday and call us terrible names, after working the problem out, when they walk in the classroom on Tuesday we do not go stiff.

THE PITHY POINT
I don't have to like your actions to like you as a person.

COMPETENCY is the fourth need. It is the need to be seen as capable. In school kids need to know that they can do the work assigned to them successfully 70% to 80% of the time if they try. Once again, the kids whose basic need is met, meaning those kids who can do the work, behave in a reasonable manner, and do the work assigned them to the best of their ability. It is the kids who can't do the work, or believe they can't do the work, who begin to cause problems. They will develop a repertoire of behaviors to make sure that their lack of ability is not exposed to you or their peers. The aggressive kids, when they're called on and don't know the answer, may make a joke, ask a way-out question, have to go to the bathroom, say something totally off the wall, or create some kind of classroom disturbance. The more passive students will use coming late to class, coming with no materials, cutting class or skipping school to avoid being exposed as incompetent. No student will sit in the classroom unable to do the work, getting failing grades on a regular basis, and say, "Oh thank you great teacher for allowing me to sit here and feel stupid."

THE PITHY POINT
There is no discipline technique that will shape up a student who cannot successfully do the work.

It is important to understand that there is no behavior management program or discipline technique that can make kids who can't do the work or believe they can't do the work behave. The solution for the behavior problems lies in providing students with work they can do. This has great implications for curriculum development and inclusion of special education students. Our role is to stop thinking in terms like "this is ninth grade English," and focus more on "can the kids in this class really do the work I'm giving them?"

WHAT STUDENTS WILL DO TO FIND COMMUNITY

When students' basic needs are not fulfilled, two things begin to happen. As we discussed in the preceding section, first their behavior will begin to slide; aggressive kids acting out and passive kids withdrawing. Second they will look for a place to belong. This need to belong is so strong that they will do whatever it takes to find a group who will accept them as a member. This is where problems begin. Let's look at the behavior of a girl who's needs were not met at home or at school.

 **IN MY D.A.R.E. T-SHIRT**

Melinda was in junior high when I knew her. She was overweight, had long mousy brown greasy hair, and a severe case of acne. She was a poor student and went to the Resource Room daily. At lunch and at recess you would usually find her alone or on the sidelines of an "in" group of kids, desparately wanting to be noticed.

There was one group of "in" girls in the school who were pretty wild. They came from money but still thought it cute to rip things off from the stores in the mall. One of them had almost gotten caught by the mall security guards and as they were talking this over at lunch, they came up with a brilliant plan. Why risk getting busted when they could find someone to do the stealing for them? And who better to ask than poor Melinda. From the way she had been hanging around them they knew they could talk her into it.

And sure enough, when asked, Melinda readily agreed. Just to be asked to go to the mall with these girls sent her heart soaring. Maybe, she thought, if she stole the clothes like they asked her to, they would really like her and begin to include her in the group's activities.

So after school off they went, Melinda wearing, of all things, her D.A.R.E. t-shirt. They entered the big department store and the girls picked out some merchandise for her to steal. They even gave her some helpful hints on how to best accomplish the task. Then they stood back and waited.

Melinda didn't get caught that day, but she didn't make any friends either. Once the girls got the merchandise, they ran off laughing. The next day at school they ignored her as usual. For as long as I knew her, the only time they paid any attention to her was when they wanted something from her. I never knew her to say no.

 WHAT'S THE POINT?

Kids who do not find a sense of family or community at home or in school, will do whatever it takes to find it elsewhere. We would hope that most kids would find their sense of community in their families. Increasingly in our society kids are coming to school without this sense of family or community. This has little to do with race, religion, or socioeconomic status. It seems to have more to do with the fragmentation taking place in our society. Not finding belonging in their families, kids then look for it in the school setting. If they do not find it at school, they turn to their peers. They will do anything; drugs, sex, theft, arson, pregnancy, even murder, to be accepted in a group they can call their family. Having been through programs like D.A.R.E. and learning to "Just Say No," while not a bad idea, do not keep kids from giving in to temptation if they do not have a strong internalized sense of self. This sense of self is developed in students when their basic needs are met at home and in school.

We cannot change what is happening in the families. We can change what is happening in the classroom. The purpose of this book is to provide ideas for fulfilling the four basic needs in our students. When the needs are fulfilled we will create a sense of family or community in the school setting. This will bond the students to us, to the school, and to a lifelong love of learning. When we don't address these needs, and the students have

THE PITHY POINT
Fulfilling students' four basic needs helps prevent drug and alcohol addiction, early pregnancy, and antisocial behavior. It's a good thing!

not had them fulfilled at home, we increase the odds for them turning to drugs, alcohol, gangs, and cults and turning on us.

THE JOURNEY TO COMMUNITY

To illustrate how powerful the need to belong or be part of a community is to all human beings (children and adults), and the profound effect it has on behavior, we (Linda and Betsy) would like to take you on a journey, a walk through an adult scenario that parallels what students face everyday in the classroom. Our goal is for you to understand, on a personal level, the importance of fulfilling the four basic needs in school.

THE JOURNEY

You have been a teacher in this school for twenty years. For twenty years your need for **INCLUSiON** has been fulfilled; you have been one of the "in" group. You have had a lot of **CONTROL**. You have been on all the important committees, and when you speak people have listened. **AFFECTION** has been no problem. You like most of the staff and everyone seems to like you. When you go in the faculty room for lunch, people gather 'round and chat. And you are so **COMPETENT**. Every evaluation has been glowing. You love working here. You will do anything for this school. You **BELONG**. This faculty is **FAMILY**. This is **COMMUNITY**.

One summer in August as you are reading the morning paper, you notice an article about your school. It says that the current principal has been transferred, and someone unknown to you has been assigned to fill the vacancy. Immediately you get a feeling of anxiety in the pit of your stomach. Some of you will even drive fifty miles out of your way to drop by the school and go in and introduce yourself to the new principal. Your friends will call this behavior "brown-nosing" or "sucking up." You call it, "getting your needs met."

The school year starts. Forget **INCLUSION**. The new principal has brought several teachers and a secretary with him, and you are no longer part of the "in" group. Forget **CONTROL**. You are no longer on any of the important committees. When you volunteer your opinion, you are told "when we want your opinion we'll ask you. In the meantime read your memos." Forget **AFFECTION**. You go in the faculty room and sit down for lunch, and people get up and walk away. And forget **COMPETENCY**. For the first time in twenty-one years your evaluation is mediocre. Forget **BELONGING.** Forget **FAMILY.** Forget **COMMUNITY.**

What is the feeling you get in the pit of your stomach? Most of the thousands of teachers we have done this exercise with, say they are now experiencing feelings of pain and anxiety. Now which way do you feel your behavior sliding? Experience has taught us that you aggressive teachers will begin to rev up and fight the new principal. You will "bad-mouth" him in the community, confront him at faculty meetings, and openly undermine him any chance you get. Those of you with more passive personalities will gather a few of your closest friends, go in the classroom, shut the door, and rip him to shreds. However the big question is, "Under these circumstances will you continue to give your all for the school?" Resoundingly the answer is always "No."

I GOT IT!
Helping kids fulfill their four basic needs is good for them and good for me.

The kids in your classroom feel exactly the same way. When their needs are fulfilled they will work with you. In fact they'll do almost anything for you. When their needs aren't fulfilled, they will work against you, either doing nothing or becoming your worst nightmare. What kind of kids do you want in your class?

CHAPTER 3

INCLUSION
A Closer Look at the First Need

IN THIS CHAPTER

- What behaviors do we see in aggressive students who don't fit in?

- How do passive students react to being one of the "outside" kids looking at the "in" kids?

- What can I do to help all students feel "in"?

Chapter 3

INCLUSION
A Closer Look at the First Need

The first need students have when two or more come together at school is the need for inclusion—to be one of the group. As we described in Chapter 2, one of the main criteria for inclusion in today's schools is clothes; to have the right look. If the student is female it helps to be perky, pretty, and thin. If the student is male it helps to be masculine, macho, and athletic. So when students enter the classroom they look

around and quickly decide whether they are "in" or not. If they feel they are "in," they can relax and attend to the business of learning. If they decide they are not "in" one of two things may happen. If students are aggressive, they will begin to act out. If students are more passive, they will begin to withdraw. Either of these classroom behaviors can lead to serious consequences in the student's life.

THE PITHY POINT
When kids don't feel "in" they begin to misbehave. Some will act out and some will withdraw, but they all will begin to go on us.

LOOKING AT AGGRESSIVE STUDENTS WHO AREN'T "IN"

The overriding need for inclusion will push aggressive kids to act out in the classroom. Take a look at how Joel, only a second grader, handled not being one of the "in" kids.

JOEL IN CHARGE

Joel was a second grade student. In the beginning he liked to come to school. However he wanted everything done his way. When the kids wouldn't give in to him, he became very angry. When the teacher gave directions, he would shout out his own ideas like alternative ways for doing each assignment. When the kids organized into groups for games during recess he would try to change the rules to suit himself. Needless to say, Joel was rejected often by his teacher and by his classmates. They saw him as unable or unwilling to compromise or adapt. Consequently he was often ignored by his teachers and excluded by his peers from their activities.

As Joel moved up the grades, he did little to adjust in order to be part of the group, so he continued to be excluded from many activities. His behavior grew more and more aggressive toward his teachers and his classmates. He became verbally abusive toward his teachers, shouting out rude remarks when they disagreed with him or ignored him. He was verbally and physically aggressive toward his peers, screaming, stomping, pushing and hitting those who refused to cooperate with him. It got to the point that some kids would play by his rules if they really wanted to play, and the others would move to another area of the playground. His teachers tended to not make eye contact with Joel, and did whatever it took to keep from entering into any kind of interaction with him.

Joel was moving farther and father from his desire to become part of his class, but he had no idea what he could do. His behavior continued to escalate.

WHAT'S THE POINT?

Aggressive students who do not feel "in" will begin to engage in verbally and/or physically aggressive behavior. Using negative words and violent behavior are some of the ways kids who don't feel "in" may choose to attract people to themselves and make themselves feel better. Dressing the opposite of what is considered "in" is another. They consider even the negative responses from their teachers and classmates better than no responses at all.

LOOKING AT PASSIVE STUDENTS WHO DON'T FIT "IN"

The need to be "in" is so strong that even the behavior of passive students will begin to go on you if they don't feel "in." Let's explore what happens when a student with a more passive personality does not feel "in."

LOUIE'S LAMENT

Louie was a tall, handsome, articulate fourth grader who had been diagnosed by his doctor as Attention Deficient. His medication, while calming him down, did nothing to change his bizarre and disruptive behavior. He did not fit in with the group. One fine spring day, Louie arrived in Linda's office at lunch time, tray in hand, and informed her that he would no longer eat in the cafeteria because "it's too noisy." He refused to join the kids on the playground, and began to isolate himself more and more in the classroom, focusing on his jewelry, clothes or school supplies. He eventually reached the point where he ceased to make eye contact.

As the year wore on both Louie's teacher and his classmates became more and more irritated by his behavior. The teacher reached the point where she was no longer willing to try to work with Louie, and made an example of him in front of others by describing his behavior in subjective terms. Each time he behaved poorly she called his mother and requested he be sent home for more medication.

Louie realized that he was finally receiving attention, however negative. He began making loud and strange sounds. His mother reported difficulty in getting him to come to school. The staff held several conferences which included parent, teacher, resource specialists, and the student, in which each seemed unwilling to modify his or her own behavior. Of course things continued to deteriorate, until Louie ceased all interaction with peers or staff. Two years later in sixth grade, Louie is on the verge of dropping out of school. The student, parents, and school personnel blame each other.

WHAT'S THE POINT?

Passive students who do not feel "in" will begin to engage in withdrawal behavior. This behavior is destructive to themselves and to their class. We all begin to wither when we are not included. Kids in the classroom engage in behaviors like coming late, coming unprepared, and without their materials. It is up to us as teachers to model acceptance of all of our students, and to go out of our way to include these students on equal terms with the rest of the group.

WAYS TO FULFILL THE NEED FOR INCLUSION

Turn to Chapter 8: Winning Ways for Inclusion. Here you will find three things: (1) techniques for changing your behavior, (2) skills to teach kids to use to change their behavior and (3) classroom activities that develop and reinforce the four basic needs. We call these **WINNING WAYS.** They have been designed specifically for ease of use with students of all ages and abilities in any school setting.

I GOT IT!
If I can help all kids feel like they are part of the group, then I'll see behavior problems decrease and academic progress increase.

18

CHAPTER 4

CONTROL
A Closer Look at the Second Need

IN THIS CHAPTER

◉ How much control can aggressive students take?

◉ How much damage can passive students do?

◉ How can I give kids some control and still maintain the control I need to run the class?

Chapter 4

CONTROL
A Closer Look at the Second Need

The second need students have when two or more come together in the classroom is the need for control—to make decisions about what's happening in their lives. Kids require some control, but not total control, in order to feel safe and secure enough to attend to the task of learning.

As described in Chapter 2, as soon as kids enter a classroom in the fall they start testing the boundaries of authority to see how much control they will have. If the power is balanced between teacher and student, the student can attend to the tasks at hand. But if students find the climate so tight that the teachers have all the control, or if they find the place loose as a goose so that they are free to do whatever they want, one of two things will happen. The more aggressive students will rev up and begin to act out, boldly taking control. The more passive students with either begin to withdraw, or take control so quietly that the teachers will not know they've been had. To neutralize the problem, teachers need to be able to strike a power balance that satisfies the student's need for control while allowing the teacher to maintain enough control to teach the class.

THE PITHY POINT
Control is like love, the more you give the more you get.

LOOKING AT AGGRESSIVE STUDENTS TAKING CONTROL

In classes where aggressive students feel they have no control, they will begin to rev up and seize it. Some pretty dangerous things can happen. Here's an example.

MRS. FRANK'S FORTRESS

Mrs. Frank's class met in a portable room outside the school building. This isolated location allowed many questionable things to happen, since few observers passed the classroom. The classroom was a hotbed of confusion, with no organization or provisions for solving students' problems. Each day students found a chalkboard filled with book titles and page numbers. If they decided not to do the work, they suffered no consequences. There was no direct instruction, no activities, no nothing happening.

Mrs. Frank's students were often discovered elsewhere without her permission, and often without her knowledge. One fateful day, one of her students became angry when he was removed from the playground for misbehavior and placed "on the wall" for the rest of recess. Later in that day he was reprimanded by Mrs. Frank when he wouldn't do his assignments in class. Suddenly, sensing a loss of control, the student left the room unnoticed and went to the auditorium, where he set a fire that burned the curtains and smoked the entire building. This was his way of taking the control he felt he needed.

WHAT'S THE POINT?

When aggressive students are not given a share of the control, they will begin to take all the control in a way that can be unsafe for themselves and others. As educators our goal is to provide students with as much control as they are capable of handling. A general rule of thumb is the older the child, the more control he/she can be expected to handle.

LOOKING AT PASSIVE STUDENTS TAKING CONTROL

In classrooms where the teachers take all the control and give none to the students, even passive students can begin to do some pretty aggressive things. Here's how a passive student tried to find some measure of control.

THE TOO-TIGHT CLASSROOM

One day as Betsy was standing duty on the steps near the lunchroom, a group of fifth grade girls came by with their hair all frizzled out. These girls belonged to a class in which the teacher had a high need for control and gave the students none. The thing he valued most was quiet. The fashion at the time among African American girls was to wear lots of ceramic beads in their hair. When Betsy noticed the girls' frizzled hair with no beads, she asked them what was going on. It tuned out that they had been shaking their heads in class, making the beads clank. The teacher, bothered by the noise, made the girls take the beads out.

A few days later the girls started a new fad. It was called "Wear a Hundred Aluminum Bracelets on Your Arm." Before long they came down to lunch with the bracelets in their pockets. Betsy asked what had happened. They said, "Our teacher said were making too much noise, and he made us take them off." A week or so later they came down carrying their shoes. "What's with the shoes?" Betsy asked. Their reply was the same as before.

So Betsy asked them, "When your teacher gets mad, what does he do?" And they described how he would screw up his face and yell, "Shut up!" Then she asked the key question: "And how many times did you girls get him to do this today?" Sly, self-satisfied looks came over their faces as they answered, "Five."

WHAT'S THE POINT?

When passive students feel they don't have some control, they begin to try to take it all. They do it in a sneaky, underhanded way so that often we don't even know we've been had. As teachers we want to give these students enough control to satisfy their needs, while at the same time, keeping enough control to do what we need to do in the classroom.

WAYS TO FULFILL THE NEED FOR CONTROL

Turn to Chapter 9: Winning Ways for Control. Here you will find three things: (1) techniques for changing your behavior, (2) skills to teach kids to use to change their behavior and (3) classroom activities that develop and reinforce the four basic needs. We call these **WINNING WAYS.** They have been designed specifically for ease of use with students of all ages and abilities in any school setting.

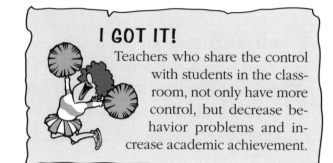

I GOT IT!
Teachers who share the control with students in the classroom, not only have more control, but decrease behavior problems and increase academic achievement.

Chapter 5

AFFECTION
A Closer Look at the Third Need

IN THIS CHAPTER

- ⚬ What happens when aggressive kids don't feel their need for affection is fulfilled?

- ⚬ How do passive kids respond where no affection is given or received?

- ⚬ What can I do to help meet all students' need for affection?

Chapter 5

AFFECTION
A Closer Look at the Third Need

The third need students have when two or more come together at school is the need for affection—to like and be liked. As described in Chapter 2, kids need to know that when they come to school they will find adults and students they can like, and who will like them. When kids do not feel liked, and if they believe there is no one whom they can like, their behavior will begin to go in one of two directions. Kids with aggressive personalities will begin to act out, while those with more passive personalities will begin to withdraw. Our goal is to interact with our students in a way that shows we like them and welcome them to liking us. It is also important to create a climate that encourages students to like each other.

LOOKING AT AGGRESSIVE KIDS WHO DON'T FEEL LIKED

THE PITHY POINT
Kids who feel loved do better in school. Kids who love others do better in school.

In classrooms where students feel they are receiving little or no affection, the aggressive ones will begin to act out. Let's take a look at the sad story of Sam.

SAM'S SAD STORY

Sam was a student who sometimes made us laugh, but more often made us angry. He assumed no responsibility for his behavior, and exhibited no control over his actions. He used a litany of choice phrases whenever the urge came upon him. Linda knew that Sam was also extremely bright, with the vocabulary of a well-educated adult, and a very mature sense of humor.

Sam's teacher was in her final year of teaching and she didn't have the energy or time to devote to this needy student. So Sam spent much of his school day in "time out" from his classroom, either in Linda's office or at home. One dark and gloomy day, Sam's teacher sent him to Linda for calling her a "f——b——." His defense was, "Can't she take a joke?" Linda said, "Apparently not, since here you are on a referral." Sam then admitted that he had called the teacher that name because "she hates me." Linda asked him why he felt that this was true, and he said, "She never smiles at me or tells me good things about myself." When asked what kind of a teacher he would like, he replied, "A teacher who laughs with us, and makes us feel happy about ourselves."

WHAT'S THE POINT?

Students need and appreciate displays of affection. We all want to be liked and to be able to like others. Teachers who show their students that they are respected, revered, and just plain liked, usually enjoy the least amount of verbal and/or physical aggression. Teachers cannot ignore disrespect, but handling it privately and in a kindly growth-producing way can transmit respect while still maintaining discipline.

LOOKING AT PASSIVE KIDS WHO LACK AFFECTION

A little affection can go a long way toward creating the right mind set for optimum learning and behavior. Even passive kids who withdraw when they feel the lack of affection can be turned around or redirected when they know that someone likes them and that it's O.K. for them to like others. Here's an example of how a small, steady stream of support can fill a student's need for affection.

RALPH'S RETREAT

Ralph was a tall lanky kid, with a shock of blond hair. He came the first day of school and immediately sat under a six place table in the corner of the room. He came out at noon, ate lunch, and immediately went back under. Linda left him alone and did not ask him to come out. In the brief interchange the two had, he seemed depressed and withdrawn.

As the days went by, he continued to come in each morning and go under the table, but by 10 am he would emerge and take his seat. He never joined the group games unless she was playing, and anytime the class left the room he stuck close by her. In the library and at gym he joined only when she stayed with the class. Linda never forced the issue. She just continued to smile and interact with him like she liked him.

In those "olden days" this school had no counselor or child development specialist; no special education programs, or special education classrooms. There was no place for Ralph to go, so he remained under the table for much of the year. While academically one would not call that year

great for Ralph, he did come to school every day, and by the end of the year was interacting more with others and attempting some school work. In other words, things at the end of the year were better than they were at the beginning. Ralph was headed in the right direction. Ralph had a relatively good year; meaning that he felt comfortable, secure and loved.

I GOT IT!
Creating a warm loving environment in the classroom is essential to good learning and good behavior.

WHAT'S THE POINT?
Most kids, including the very passive kids, will begin to respond to signs of affection. Just

25

because kids appear shy or withdrawn doesn't mean they don't have a need to like and be liked. As in a case like Ralph's, it is important to be aware that progress is often measured in very tiny steps. Because it takes about one month for every year we are old to internalize a behavior change if we are serious about it, we often may not see the behavior change we are working for in the year we have the kid. The point to remember is that we are planting the seed and have to have faith that someday it will grow.

WAYS TO FULFILL THE NEED FOR AFFECTION

 Turn to Chapter 10: Winning Ways for Affection. Here you will find three things: (1) techniques for changing your behavior, (2) skills to teach kids to use to change their behavior and (3) classroom activities that develop and reinforce the four basic needs. We call these **WINNING WAYS.** They have been designed specifically for ease of use with students of all ages and abilities in any school setting.

Chapter 6

COMPETENCY
A Closer Look at the Fourth Need

IN THIS CHAPTER

- ⟲ What kinds of behavior do we see from aggressive kids who feel incompetent?

- ⟲ What will passive kids do if they don't feel competent?

- ⟲ In a classroom with a wide range of abilities, how can I help all kids feel competent?

27

Chapter 6

COMPETENCY
A Closer Look at the Fourth Need

The fourth need students have when two or more come together in the classroom is the need for competency—to be seen as being capable. As described in Chapter 2, if students find that they cannot do their class work successfully seventy to eighty percent of the time when they try, their behavior will begin to go. As with the previous three needs, the aggressive students will act out and the passive kids will withdraw.

LOOKING AT AGGRESSIVE STUDENTS WHO FEEL THEY AREN'T COMPETENT

The more aggressive students who don't experience success in the class room will begin to act out, usually until they get kicked out of class. Here's an example of an aggressive student who didn't experience success in the classroom.

THE PITHY POINT
Students who experience failure become failures. Students who experience success become successful.

THE KID WHO WORKED THE SYSTEM

Jerid didn't learn to read in the first grade. He came to school all excited, as most first-graders do, and wanted to learn to read, but as the year progressed he did not catch on, and he got further and further behind. By second grade he was tested and labeled "learning disabled" (today called ADHD). Jerid was sent to Chapter 1 classes and then to Resource, where his time increased each year until by middle school he was spending most of his day in Resource.

Jerid did not like Resource. He said only dumb kids went there, and he began to work the situation. He loudly refused to do his work and called the assignments "baby stuff." He wandered the room, hitting kids with his pencil, grabbing their papers, or knocking their books on the floor. His favorite statement was, "I'm not going to do anything, and you can't make me." Jerid began to spend lots of time in the detention room and at home on suspension.

By high school, "mainstreaming" had become popular for ADHD kids, so Jerid's time in Resource was reduced and he was scheduled into many regular classes. Again, he quickly learned to work the system. He would walk into class, snarl at the teacher, throw a few put-downs at other students, slam his body into a chair, and ask loudly, "What dumb sh—are we going to do today?" If that didn't get him out of class, he would insult the teacher or pick a fight with another student.

By his junior year he had figured out how to be out of school most of the time, and was well on his way to being permanently removed. He still was not able to do any of the regularly assigned classwork successfully.

Betsy was visiting one day as he sauntered into class. Kids gathered around him, talking excitedly. He was the center of attention, and they all seemed glad to see him. Betsy asked where he had been, thinking it must have been some great trip. "I've been on a three-day suspension," he said. "What for?" she asked. "For not going to Saturday School," he replied. She asked him to explain.

"It works like this," he said. "First I come to school and act up in class until the teacher gets mad and sends me to in-school suspension. Then I don't show up for in-school suspension, and the vice-principal gets mad and sends me to Saturday School. Then I don't show up for Saturday School, and the principal gets mad and suspends me for three days. Then I go home for three days, come back, and start all over. It really is no problem once you learn to play the game."

WHAT'S THE POINT?

Students need to be able to do the work assigned. It is important that when they come to school they can to do their work successfully 70% to 80% of the time if they try. When we construct lessons that teach each concept in many different ways, we generally stumble upon a way that clicks with each kid. Remember, Jerid came to school wanting to learn. The fact that he did not respond to the way he was being taught made him feel incompetent, which further impaired his ability to learn.

LOOKING AT WHAT HAPPENS TO PASSIVE KIDS WHO DON'T FEEL COMPETENT

When the more passive students feel incompetent, they will begin to withdraw until they can drop out of school. Let's look at Jenny's seven year journey.

JENNY'S JOURNEY

Jenny was a fifth grader now. She had come to our school seven years ago in pre-kindergarten. Then she was a bright, smiling four year old, eager to come to school because she had heard great things about it. For the first two years she seemed like every other kid. It wasn't until first grade that the teachers began to notice that she was having a difficult time understanding concepts such as color, numbers and letters. For the first time in her life Jenny was beginning to experience failure.

The teacher, like most of us, had her hands full with 27 other students. She had little time to give Jenny extra help. Her mother was informed of the struggles, and vowed to help her at home, but she did not want Jenny retained. The teacher referred Jenny for testing and as often is the case, she was diagnosed as a "slow learner" and didn't qualify for special help. As she moved on up the grades she experienced more and more difficulty learning academic skills. The academic gap between the other students and Jenny grew. Kids began to tease her, and she withdrew into herself. By fifth grade the regular classroom work that she was given was completely beyond her grasp. She often skipped school, played sick, and tried everything she could to keep from coming. When she was there she was too tired to work, her pencil was lost, she had no paper, etc. She was negative about herself and was on her way to dropping out of school.

WHAT'S THE POINT?

Students need to be able to do the work assigned. More and more kids like Jenny are coming into our classrooms. Because they withdraw they are much easier to overlook than those who act out. However, whether acting out or withdrawing, all kids have the need to be seen as competent in our classrooms. Therefore, it's imperative that we construct lessons that kids can complete successfully. Recognizing that it is often overwhelming to prepare special work for certain kids, in the end it pays off.

I GOT IT!
Kids who are taught at their ability level increase their level of ability.

WAYS TO FULFILL THE NEED FOR COMPETENCY

Turn to Chapter 11: Winning Ways for Competency. Here you will find three things: (1) techniques for changing your behavior, (2) skills to teach kids to use to change their behavior and (3) classroom activities that develop and reinforce the four basic needs. We call these **WINNING WAYS.** They have been designed specifically for ease of use with students of all ages and abilities in any school setting.

Enough of this theory, let's get down to the " How do I do it?"

CHAPTER 7

HOW TO USE THIS BOOK

IN THIS CHAPTER

- Is it possible to determine if kids' needs in school are being met by examining their behavior and mine?

- Once I understand what's lacking, how do I make things better?

- Are **WINNING WAYS** really the answer, or are they just another add-on?

- Change! Does it have to be as difficult as I think it is?

Chapter 7
FIVE WAYS TO USE THIS BOOK

Now that you understand the four basic needs that all students have when they come to us in the school setting, the question becomes, "How can I use this knowledge to my advantage?" In this chapter we, Betsy and Linda, have presented you with a process for determining how well the needs of the students in your classroom are being met. We have provided you with surveys for examining your behavior and the behavior of your students. We will show you how to use this information to select appropriate **WINNING WAYS** *to address need deficiencies. In other words we will guide you in selecting practical, exciting, effective lessons to address each of the basic needs. We will also alert you to some of the pitfalls as well as some of the joys of implementing change in your classroom.*

FIVE WAYS TO USE THIS BOOK

WAY ONE: TAKE OUR WORD FOR IT

After having read the previous chapters, some teachers just accept the fact that students come to school looking to satisfy, in this order, the needs of **INCLUSION, CONTROL, AFFECTION**, and **COMPETENCY**. These teachers look at their lesson plans and analyze them as to the four basic needs. They use the four **WINNING WAYS** sections in this book to draw ideas for daily and/or weekly lessons so that they can specifically teach to each of the four needs on a regular basis.

If you fall into this category, go straight to the **PLANNING SHEET** (Worksheet 8) and follow the directions given in the section of this chapter called **Making a Plan and Following the Plan.**

I GOT IT!
I've read enough, I'm going straight for the **WINNING WAYS.**

WAY TWO: TEACHER SELF SURVEY

The second approach to using the information regarding the four basic needs is to carefully take a look at your behavior. The authors have provided you with a simple "complete the sentence" survey called **TEACHER SELF SURVEY** (Worksheet 1). The idea is to sit down in a quiet time and space, either alone or with one or two close friends, and as honestly as possible, answer each of the questions. Then looking at your answers, formulate some conclusions about what you are teaching in the classroom. The bottom line question for you is, **"Am I, on a regular basis, teaching to each of the four basic needs in my classroom?"**

If you believe there is any room at all for improvement, go to the **PLANNING SHEET** (Worksheet 8) and follow the directions given in the section of this chapter called **Making a Plan and Following the Plan.**

THE PITHY POINT
As difficult as it is to look at our own behavior, it is absolutely necessary if we want to be the best we can be.

WAY THREE: STUDENT SURVEY: COMPLETE THE SENTENCE

The third approach for using the information we have presented about the four basic needs is to administer a "complete the sentence" student survey. The authors have provided you with a **STUDENT SURVEY: COMPLETE THE SENTENCE** (Worksheet 2).

Experience has shown that, if possible, it best to have someone other than the classroom teacher administer the survey. It even helps if the classroom teacher can leave the room during the process. Students seem to be a little more honest in their answers if their teacher isn't present. It also helps if you ask the students to put down their pencils and then read the entire survey to them, regardless of grade level, before giving them the signal to begin. The authors never would have thought this, but found it helpful to be able to clarify and answer questions item by item before turning students loose on the survey.

After administering the **STUDENT SURVEY: COMPLETE THE SENTENCE** (Worksheet 2), tally the results using the **STUDENT SURVEY: COMPLETE THE SENTENCE SUMMARY SHEET** (Worksheet 3). Once you determine the areas that need to be addressed, go straight to the **PLANNING SHEET** (Worksheet 8), and all you have left to do is make your plan and follow your plan.

WAY FOUR: STUDENT SURVEY: MULTIPLE CHOICE

The fourth approach for using the information presented in this book is to do a multiple choice survey with your students. The authors have provided you with the **STUDENT SURVEY: MULTIPLE CHOICE** (Worksheet 4). The advantages for using this survey instead of the **STUDENT SURVEY: COMPLETE THE SENTENCE** are that it is easier to administer and easier to tally. The disadvantage is that students in some schools and some communities tend to be less truthful about how they really feel when using multiple choice. The authors found this was particularly true with middle school students.

THE PITHY POINT
If we really want to know how well things are going in the classroom, we need to ask the people who are sitting in the chairs every day.

The authors have also provided you with a **STUDENT SURVEY: MULTIPLE CHOICE SUMMARY SHEET** (Worksheet 5). Once you have administered the survey to the students, use this form to tally the results. The questions are grouped by basic need so that you can study the results and draw some conclusions about which needs students feel are being satisfied and which are not. Now use the **PLANNING SHEET** (Worksheet 8) and make a plan to address the deficient needs.

THE PITHY POINT
It is important to teach to the four basic needs on a regular basis whether or not they show up deficient on the surveys.

WAY FIVE: SCHOOL COMMUNITY SURVEY

A fifth approach for using the information presented here is to go beyond the individual classroom and focus on the school as a whole. The authors have provided you with the **SCHOOL COMMUNITY SURVEY** (Worksheet 6) which can be used with a variety of populations; students, school employees, parents, community members, and others. The purpose is to determine how well the school is functioning as a family or community and to identify the basic needs that need to be addressed in order to make it a welcoming place for all populations.

As with the other surveys, administer the survey, then compile the results, using the **SCHOOL COMMUNITY SURVEY SUMMARY SHEET** (Worksheet 7). Once you have identified the areas in need of attention, formulate a plan using the **PLANNING SHEET** (Worksheet 8). While the **WINNING WAYS** are not specifically written for whole school application, any of them can be implemented on a school-wide basis. For example, while it's not feasible to have someone standing by the front door of the building to welcome each person as they come in the door like you welcome kids into your classroom each day, it is possible to take the concept and focus on how people do great visitors to the building.

I GOT IT!
I made my plan. Now all I need to do is follow my plan.

MAKING A PLAN AND FOLLOWING THE PLAN

Using a copy of the **PLANNING SHEET** (Worksheet 8), check the basic needs that you have determined need to be addressed in your classroom. Then turn to the specific **WINNING WAY** section of this book, the section that speaks to the need you have found deficient, and select a number of **WINNING WAYS** you plan to try. Record the page number and the title of each **WINNING WAY** you have selected on your **PLANNING SHEET** (Worksheet 8). Set some goals for yourself by assigning a date for teaching each **WINNING WAY** selected. Now you are ready to discover the joy that comes when you help students begin to fulfill their basic needs.

WINNING WAYS

WINNING WAYS are (1) techniques for changing your behavior, (2) skills to teach kids to use to change their behavior, and (3) classroom activities that develop and reinforce the four basic needs. We have designed them specifically for use with students of all ages and abilities and in any school setting. Please feel free to copy any of the material for your personal use and adapt all ideas and concepts to your grade level, subject, and personal focus.

On each **WINNING WAY** sheet you will find several icons to help you quickly identify each section.

| INCLUSION | CONTROL | AFFECTION | COMPETENCY |

The worksheets are divided into chapters for each of the four basic needs; **INCLUSION, CONTROL, AFFECTION, COMPETENCY.** At the top of each **WINNING WAY** sheet you will find the four icons shown above.

 A double check mark underneath an icon indicates that particular need is addressed in the following activity. Often an activity will address more than one of the basic needs. The secondary need(s) addressed are noted with single check marks (✓) under the icon(s).

 WHAT'S THE POINT?
This icon is found at the beginning of each **WINNING WAY** sheet and indicates the activity's purpose.

 DESCRIPTION OF THE TECHNIQUE.
This icon indicates the procedure. Here we have the "how-to-do-it" part of the **WINNING WAY.**

 PLEASE NOTE!
Here we share our thoughts on the procudures. They usually cover ideas regarding the procedure that we have learned the hard way.

 THOUGHTS FOR USING THIS WINNING WAY NEXT TIME.
This icon is found above a blank space on the page that is provided for you to use to make personal observations, notations, ideas, and thoughts for the next time you use the **WINNING WAY.**

 This icon indicates a specific suggestion, fact, or idea.

NOTHING ENDURES BUT CHANGE. LET'S ENJOY IT.

There is an old saying that goes, "Things tend to get worse before they get better." Change is like this. You're humming along doing your teaching thing. It is going fairly well, but in the back of your mind you have the feeling that it could be better. One day you discover this book and you say, "There are some great ideas in here. I think I'll try a few." So you survey yourself, you survey your class, you make a plan, and you teach a couple of the **WINNING WAYS.** You have a few successes. Some of the kids actually say, "That was fun." Then you have some not-so-successful experiences. You get comments like, "What book did you just read? Did you go to some seminar? Are you trying to use psychology on us? That was a dumb idea. When are you going back to your old way of teaching?"

You are now experiencing what the authors call "the dip of change." This is where things get worse before they get better. More importantly, this is the moment that separates the progressive more innovative teachers from those who are just "doing their job." You progressive teachers will continue to work to fulfill students' basic needs using the **WINNING WAYS** until you reach a point where you and the students are comfortable with the new ideas and ways of doing things. You and your students will now have come out of the "dip of change" and will have risen to a higher level of functioning. Those of you who don't tolerate being out of your comfort zone will quickly drop **WINNING WAYS** and go back to "business as usual." You and your students will not rise to a higher level.

I GOT IT!
True leaders work through the "dip of change" to achieve their goals.

True leaders have a vision or a picture in their heads of what they are trying to accomplish. Our vision, the one we have in our heads as we write this book, is to teach students to take responsibility for their learning and their behavior, while experiencing with students the joy that comes from working and learning together. Addressing the four basic needs on a daily basis is the best way we have found to achieve these goals.

If we experience some discomfort as we try new ideas, it is a small price to pay for the satisfaction and joy that will eventually be theirs and ours.

WINNING WAYS
WORKSHEETS

TEACHER SELF SURVEY

DIRECTIONS: Briefly answer each of the following questions. Be very specific about listing actual behaviors that you use in each area. Can't think of many? No problem. That's what **WINNING WAYS** are for. Reflect upon your answers and record your conclusions as to how well you feel you are addressing the four basic needs. Then turn to the **PLANNING SHEET** and make a plan to address the areas in need of improvement.

INCLUSION

How do I help each kid fit in?

1. _____
2. _____
3. _____
4. _____

How do I model acceptance of each student?

1. _____
2. _____
3. _____
4. _____

What behaviors do I use that might send the message that certain kids are not "in" with me?

1. _____
2. _____
3. _____
4. _____

CONCLUSIONS: What comes to you after reviewing your answers on this page? Record your thoughts in the space below. Do you feel you could do more to make each student feel "in"? If so, turn to the **WINNING WAYS** section on **INCLUSION** and select some activities that appeal to you. Record them on the **PLANNING SHEET** (Figure 8) and begin to include them in your daily teaching.

_____
_____
_____
_____
_____

TEACHER SELF SURVEY (Page 2)

CONTROL

How do I give students control in the curriculum area?

1. _____
2. _____
3. _____
4. _____

How do I give students control in the area of behavior?

1. _____
2. _____
3. _____
4. _____

What behaviors do I use that might send the message that I am making most of the decisions?

1. _____
2. _____
3. _____
4. _____

CONCLUSIONS: What comes to you after reviewing your answers on this page? Record your thoughts in the space below. Do you feel you could do more to give each student a true sense of control regarding curriculum and behavior? If so, turn to the **WINNING WAYS** section on **CONTROL** and select some activities that appeal to you. Record them on the **PLANNING SHEET (Figure** 8) and begin to include them in your daily teaching.

_____
_____
_____
_____
_____
_____
_____
_____
_____
_____

TEACHER SELF SURVEY (Page 3)

AFFECTION

What behaviors do I use that send the message to students that I like them regardless of their behavior?

1. _____
2. _____
3. _____
4. _____

What behaviors do I use that send the message to students that I can be their friend as well as their teacher?

1. _____
2. _____
3. _____
4. _____

What behaviors do I use that might send the message that I don't like a student?

1. _____
2. _____
3. _____
4. _____

CONCLUSIONS: What comes to you after reviewing your answers on this page? Record your thoughts in the space below. Do you feel you could do more to demonstrate that you like each student, regardless of behavior and that it's OK for each kid to like you if they want to. If so, turn to the **WINNING WAYS** section on **AFFECTION** and select some activities that appeal to you. Record them on the **PLANNING SHEET** (Figure 8) and begin to include them in your daily teaching.

_____
_____
_____
_____
_____
_____
_____
_____
_____

TEACHER SELF SURVEY (Page 4)

COMPETENCY

What do I do to adjust the curriculum so that every kid in my class can experience success daily?

1. _____

2. _____

3. _____

4. _____

How do I insure that my special needs kids are experiencing success with curriculum in my classroom?

1. _____

2. _____

3. _____

4. _____

What do I do that might be sending the message that "if you can't do the lesson I present, it's your problem?"

1. _____

2. _____

3. _____

4. _____

CONCLUSIONS: What comes to you after reviewing your answers on this page? Record your thoughts in the space below. Do you feel you could do more to design lessons so that each kid in your classroom can experience success? If so, turn to the **WINNING WAYS** section on **COMPETENCY** and select some activities that appeal to you. Record them on the **PLANNING SHEET** (Figure 8) and begin to include them in your daily teaching.

_____

_____

_____

_____

_____

_____

STUDENT SURVEY: COMPLETE THE SENTENCES

1. To be one of the popular kids in the school I need to _____

   _____

2. To have a group of friends who accept me I need to _____

   _____

3. I get to make decisions when I am in the following places at school_____

   _____

4. When I am at school I get to make decisions about the following things _____

   _____

5. In school I can tell other kids like me when they _____

   _____

6. In school I can tell teachers like me when they _____

   _____

7. It is easiest for me to learn in class when I _____

   _____

8. It is easiest for me to learn in class when the teacher _____

   _____

9. The things I like most about coming to school are:

   1. _____

   2. _____

   3. _____

10. Some of the things I worry about when I come to school are:

   1. _____

   2. _____

   3. _____

STUDENT SURVEY: COMPLETE THE SENTENCES
SUMMARY SHEET

INCLUSION	CONTROL	AFFECTION	COMPETENCY
Question #1	Question #3	Question #5	Question #7
Question #2	Question #4	Question #6	Question #8

The data suggests I might want to focus on: _____

_____

_____

_____

_____

_____

_____

STUDENT SURVEY: COMPLETE THE SENTENCES
SUMMARY SHEET (Page 2)

THINGS I LIKE	THINGS I WORRY ABOUT
Question #9	Question #10

The data suggests I might want to focus on: _____

_____

_____

_____

_____

_____

_____

_____

_____

_____

_____

Now turn to the PLANNING SHEET (Figure 8) and prepare your plan.

STUDENT SURVEY: MULTIPLE CHOICE

DIRECTIONS: Think of yourself in this school, going to class, eating lunch, being in the halls, on the playground; just doing all the things that you do during the school day. Then respond to the statements below by checking *most of the time, some of the time, or hardly ever.*

IN THIS SCHOOL KIDS FEEL THAT:	*most of the time*	*some of the time*	*hardly ever*
1. They fit in wherever they go in the building.	_____	_____	_____
2. They get to make some decisions about what happens to them when they get caught misbehaving.	_____	_____	_____
3. The teachers like the students.	_____	_____	_____
4. The teachers think the kids are really smart and can learn.	_____	_____	_____
5. They have to act and dress a certain way to be accepted.	_____	_____	_____
6. They get to make some decisions about what happens in the classroom.	_____	_____	_____
7. The kids like each other.	_____	_____	_____
8. Kids who go for special help like Chapter 1 and tutoring are considered the dumb kids.	_____	_____	_____
9. People show that they like each other by doing things like giving hugs and high fives.	_____	_____	_____
10. They feel that they can do the work that the teachers give them.	_____	_____	_____
11. Others reject them if they don't dress and act a certain way.	_____	_____	_____
12. Adults really listen to what they have to say.	_____	_____	_____
13. People show that they like each other with words.	_____	_____	_____
14. It is OK to be one of the smart kids.	_____	_____	_____

STUDENT SURVEY: MULTIPLE CHOICE
SUMMARY SHEET

IN THIS SCHOOL KIDS FEEL THAT:	*most of the time*	*some of the time*	*hardly ever*
INCLUSION			
1. They fit in wherever they go in the building.	_____	_____	_____
5. They have to act and dress a certain way to be accepted.	_____	_____	_____
11. Others reject them if they don't dress and act a certain way.	_____	_____	_____
CONTROL			
2. They get to make some decisions about what happens to them when they get caught misbehaving.	_____	_____	_____
6. They get to make some decisions about what happens to them in the classroom.	_____	_____	_____
12. Adults really listen to what they have to say.	_____	_____	_____
AFFECTION			
3. The teachers like the students.	_____	_____	_____
7. The kids like each other.	_____	_____	_____
13. People show they like each other with words.	_____	_____	_____
9. People show that they like each other by doing things like giving hugs and high fives.	_____	_____	_____
COMPETENCY			
4. The teachers think the kids are smart and can really learn.	_____	_____	_____
8. Kids who go for special help like Chapter 1 and tutoring are considered the dumb kids.	_____	_____	_____
14. It is OK to be one of the really smart kids.	_____	_____	_____
10. They can do the work that the teachers give them.	_____	_____	_____

The data suggests that I might want to: _____

_____

_____

_____

_____

_____

_____

_____

Now turn to the PLANNING SHEET (Figure 8) and prepare your plan.

SCHOOL COMMUNITY SURVEY

Check One: ☐ Student ☐ School Employee ☐ Parent ☐ Community Member

Directions: Thinking in terms of your relationship to this school, answer each question using a few words or a short phrase. Please use general terms instead of specific names when possible For example, use "some teachers" instead if Mrs. Morrison and Mr. Stark. All responses are anonymous and will be used to improve the climate in the school. Thank you for taking your time to help us improve.

1.   Who are the "in" people here? _____

2.   What makes people feel accepted here? _____

3.   What makes people feel rejected here? _____

4.   What does a person have to do be accepted here? _____

5.   Who has the power in this school? _____

6.   How are the decisions made? _____

7.   What does a person have to do to influence decisions? _____

     _____

8.   What makes this school a friendly place? _____

9.   What makes this school an unfriendly place? _____

10. How is affection expressed here? _____

11. What makes people feel smart or capable here? _____

     _____

12. What makes people feel that they aren't smart or capable? _____

     _____

13. What does a person have to do here to be seen as smart or capable? _____

     _____

14. About being part of this school community I feel (circle one):

          GREAT   GOOD   OK   SO-SO   BAD

SCHOOL COMMUNITY SURVEY
SUMMARY SHEET

INCLUSION	CONTROL	AFFECTION	COMPETENCY
Question #1-4	Question #5-7	Question #8-10	Question #11-13

Class _____

SCHOOL COMMUNITY SURVEY
SUMMARY SHEET (Page 2)

I FEEL...				
GREAT	GOOD	OK	SO-SO	BAD

The data suggests we might want to focus on: _____

_____

_____

_____

_____

_____

_____

_____

_____

_____

_____

_____

_____

_____

_____

_____

_____

Now turn to the PLANNING SHEET (Figure 8) and prepare your plan.

— Worksheet 7 —

PLANNING SHEET

NEEDS TO ADDRESS	WINNING WAYS TO EXPERIMENT WITH		
	PAGE	WINNING WAYS	DATE
☐ INCLUSION *(the need to be "in")*			
☐ CONTROL *(the need to make decisions)*			
☐ AFFECTION *(the need to like and be liked)*			
☐ COMPETENCY *(the need to be seen as capable)*			

CHAPTER 8

WINNING WAYS

for

INCLUSION

MODEL, MODEL, MODEL
Do As I Do

WHAT'S THE POINT?

⟳ **To model on a daily basis the behaviors I want to see in the kids in front of me.**
Teachers who model the behaviors they want, such as being courteous, respecting others, and remaining in control of themselves tend to have classes that exhibit the same behaviors.

DESCRIPTION OF THE TECHNIQUE:

⟳ **Simply show your students through your own behavior how to act in the classroom. Some examples are:**
- Talking in a quiet voice.
- Listening to others.
- Being helpful to others.
- Treating students with respect, regardless of behavior.
- Making eye contact.
- Smiling.
- Keeping personal materials neat and tidy.
- Respecting others' property.
- Treating every student like they're your best friend.
- Leading with empathy.
- Using the problem solving model.
- Showing an interest in every student.
- Using "can do" messages instead of "can't do" messages.

PLEASE NOTE!

⟳ **Modeling is the most powerful behavior you can use in the classroom. Students do as we do, not as we say.** So save your breath and start doing.

THOUGHTS...

_____
_____
_____
_____
_____
_____
_____
_____
_____
_____
_____

EYE CONTACT
Bonding the Student to You

 WHAT'S THE POINT?

🌀 **To build the relationship or bond the student to you.** Speaking directly to the eyes when you have a smile or at least a semi-smile on your face sends the message "I like you." It also ups the odds for the message being received and acted upon in a positive manner.

 DESCRIPTION OF THE TECHNIQUE:

🌀 **At the door.**
Stand in the doorway at the beginning and end of each period or each transition time. As students come in or leave, for one brief moment look into their eyes like they are the only student you see.

🌀 **In the classroom.**
Walk toward a student and get as close as feels comfortable to you and the student before speaking. Look directly into the eyes of the student as you speak.

🌀 **Around the building.**
Use this same procedure in the hall, the cafeteria, the playground and all other areas of the school.

 PLEASE NOTE!

🌀 **Never demand a student look at you.** Just look where the eyes are. When enough trust has developed, the student will look at you.

 **THOUGHTS...**

_____

_____

_____

_____

_____

_____

_____

_____

_____

_____

_____

_____

_____

INCLUSION CONTROL  AFFECTION  COMPETENCY

DECORATING THE ROOM

 WHAT'S THE POINT?

- **To decorate the room in a way that shouts "This is our classroom."** Students spend upwards of five hours a day, five days a week in their classrooms. By helping them make it theirs, you will increase the odds that they will want to be there.

 DESCRIPTION OF THE TECHNIQUE:

- **Some thoughts for getting started are:**
  - Display or hang up information that helps students understand who you are. Some ideas are:
    - Display pictures of your hobbies, vacation experiences, etc.
    - Share pictures of your family, home, etc.
  - Save space for students to put up something about themselves the first week of school. Some ideas are:
    - Designate one board for student work for the entire school year.
    - Divide bulletin boards so that each student has his/her own display area.
  - Display things that reflect the age, grade level, and interests of your students.
  - Don't overdecorate, especially with younger kids. It can be overwhelming and distracting.

- **Some thoughts for maintaining.**
  - Display current class projects and papers.
  - Change the displays frequently.
  - Keep the classroom tidy at all times.
  - Ask students for ideas for displays.
  - Let students put up the displays.

 PLEASE NOTE!

- **Things tend to pile up in the rush of the school year.** Every few weeks clean house and redo with fresh and new. Think of yourself as a department store. While Christmas decorations are often put up by Halloween, they are always taken down the day after Christmas.

THOUGHTS...

_____
_____
_____
_____
_____
_____
_____

 INCLUSION  CONTROL  AFFECTION COMPETENCY

BUILDING CLASS IDENTITY

WHAT'S THE POINT?

⑥ To bond the students to you, to each other, and to the school by developing a unique class identity.

DESCRIPTION OF THE TECHNIQUE:

• Design a class flag that can hang outside the classroom door and be carried to school events.
• Write a class song and/or class cheer that can be used in the room and at assemblies.
• Make a time capsule that can be opened at the end of the school year.
• Select class colors, a class motto, a class logo, etc.
• Develop a class charter and/or constitution.
• Develop class rules and/or write a class creed.

⑥ **Variation**

Do these activities on a school-wide level. See the next pages for some examples.

PLEASE NOTE!

⑥ **The more classes involved in this process, the more pride the students will have in the school.** However, don't let the fact that you're the only classroom doing this hold you back.

THOUGHTS...

_____
_____
_____
_____
_____
_____
_____
_____
_____
_____
_____
_____
_____
_____
_____

VERNON SCHOOL CREED

I am. . .
A good learner.
On time daily.
Taking care of myself.
Doing my part to
keep Vernon clean and safe.
Treating others as I
would like to be treated.

by Vernon Students

VERNON SCHOOL CHEER

Vernon owls
Vernon owls
Vernon owls are proud.
So let's give a howl
we are Vernon owls.
Rah Rah
Hoot Hoot
Vernon owls.
Rah Rah
Hoot Hoot
We're Vernon owls.

by May Chin
5th Grade Teacher
Vernon School

VERNON SCHOOL SONG

Vernon we love you
Vernon we love you
We love you in the springtime
and the fall.
Vernon we love you
Vernon we love you
We love you best of all.

Our colors are red and white.
Our eyes are clear and bright.
We're happy and we are proud,
as we sing our song out loud.

Vernon we love you
Vernon we love you
We love you in the springtime
and the fall.
Vernon we love you
Vernon we love you
We love you best of all.

by Lillian Whitlow
5th Grade Teacher
Vernon School

STUDENTS INTERVIEWING STUDENTS
Getting to Know Each Other

WHAT'S THE POINT?

⊚ **To help students get to know each other better by interviewing one another.** Don't forget, the more people get to know each other, the more they tend to understand and even like each other.

DESCRIPTION OF THE TECHNIQUE:

⊚ **Provide each student with an interview sheet (see following page).**

⊚ **Form or allow students to form pairs for interviewing.**

⊚ **When the process is complete, pull the class back together and...**

Variation
• Have the students introduce to the class the person they have interviewed.

Variation
• Have the students write a paragraph summarizing the information. These can be posted or read to the class.

THOUGHTS...

_____
_____
_____
_____
_____
_____
_____
_____
_____
_____
_____
_____
_____
_____
_____
_____
_____
_____
_____

STUDENTS INTERVIEWING STUDENTS

1. Who was your teacher last year? _____

2. What is your favorite subject at school? _____

3. What kind of music do you like best? _____

4. What do you like to do after school? _____

5. What is your favorite television show? _____

6. What is your favorite food? _____

7. Do you have any brothers or sisters? _____ Names _____

8. Do you like to buy lunch or bring lunch? _____

7. Can you do the Macarena? _____

8. Do you remember your first grade teacher's name? _____

9. When is your birthday? _____

10. Can your roller blade? _____

11. Do you have a pet? _____ What is it? _____

12. Name three special things about yourself: _____

13. What is your favorite color? _____

14. Who is your hero? _____

15. What kind of music do you like best? _____

 INCLUSION  CONTROL  AFFECTION  COMPETENCY

✓✓   ✓

BUILDING THE WEB
A Name Game

 WHAT'S THE POINT?

ⓖ **To engage students in activities that force them to interact with each other and learn each others' names.** This helps students get to know each others' names and helps develop a more positive classroom climate.

 DESCRIPTION OF THE TECHNIQUE:

ⓖ **Building the Web**

Get a ball of yarn and put the students in a circle. Holding the ball of yarn, state your name, and the name of a student in the circle. Throw the ball to that student. Have that student state his/her name and the name of another student. He/she then throws the ball to that student. Make sure students hang onto the yarn before throwing the ball to the next student. Continue this process until the ball has been thrown to every student. You will now have a giant web. Before letting go of the yarn discuss with the students ways in which we are interconnected in the classroom.

ⓖ **Variation**

As students get to know each other better first, before throwing the ball, have them state the name of each student already holding the yarn.

ⓖ **Variation**

As students get to know each other even better, use categories instead of names. Some suggestions are hobbies, interests, positive comments, something personal, etc.

THOUGHTS…

_____
_____
_____
_____
_____
_____
_____
_____
_____
_____
_____
_____
_____
_____
_____
_____
_____

FIND SOMEONE WHO

WHAT'S THE POINT?

⊚ **To force students to interact with each other and to learn more about each other.**
The more students know about each other, the more they tend like to each other and to
get along. This is called building harmony in the classroom.

DESCRIPTION OF THE TECHNIQUE:

⊚ **This is a whole group activity that can be used at the beginning of the year and
anytime throughout the year.**
• Create a **FIND SOMEONE WHO** sheet (see following pages for examples).

⊚ **Explain directions to students:**
• At the signal, find "someone who" has done one of the following things listed
below. Write the person's name on the blank beside the statement. Use each
name only once.
• Give students 5 to 7 minutes to do the activity.
• Call the group to attention. Ask for questions, comments, or funny stories related
to doing the activity.

PLEASE NOTE!

⊚ **Caution.** Control yourself. Do not ask, "Who got the most blanks filled?" This is not
a competition. Making it competitive defeats the whole purpose.
⊚ **Bonanza!** This activity can be used with curriculum material (see following pages for
examples).

THOUGHTS...

_____
_____
_____
_____
_____
_____
_____
_____
_____
_____
_____
_____
_____
_____
_____

FIND SOMEONE WHO

_____ loves to read.

_____ likes hamburgers.

_____ has freckles.

_____ has on a green shirt.

_____ is taller than me.

_____ is shorter than me.

_____ is left-handed.

_____ loves ice cream.

_____ has on shoes that buckle.

_____ loves to play kick ball.

_____ went fishing this summer.

_____ was in your class last year.

_____ has had a broken arm.

_____ loves vegetables.

_____ can swim.

_____ likes school.

FIND SOMEONE WHO

Find "Someone Who" has done one of these activities listed below. Write the person's name in the blank beside the statement. Use each name only once. Good Luck !!!!!!!!!!!

_____ WATCHES CARTOONS

_____ WENT OUT NEW YEARS EVE

_____ HAS PLAYED A GAME OF CHECKERS

_____ PLAYS SPORTS

_____ LIKES PRINCE

_____ HAS SEEN BEAVIS & BUTTHEAD HIT AMERICA

_____ HAS LITTLE BROTHERS AND SISTERS

_____ LIKES RAP MUSIC

_____ HAS A FRIEND IN CLASS

_____ WAS BORN IN OREGON

_____ LIKES CHINESE FOOD

FIND SOMEONE WHO

(a math class example)

Move about the classroom and find "someone who" has each of the following categories. Enter their name and the number on the line. One person can be put in more than one category. Fill as many blanks as you can. It helps to give students time to figure out which categories they can sign before beginning.

_____ Has an address that is a 4 digit even number.

_____ Has an address that is a 5 digit number divisible by 2 and 5.

_____ Has a phone number that is divisible by 3, all 7 digits.

_____ Has a telephone number in which the last four digits are within 1500 of the last 4 digits of their zip code.

_____ Has a locker combination in which the sum of all three numbers is greater than 60.

_____ Has a birth date that is prime.

_____ Has a social security number in which the sum of the odd digits is greater than the sum of the even digits.

_____ Has a favorite radio station whose location on the dial is an even number.

_____ Has a license plate number on one of the family autos that is divisible by 6.

_____ Has an address that alternates odd and even digits.

FIND SOMEONE WHO

(an introduction to a health lesson)

Circulate and find "someone who" has experienced one of the situations listed below, then write their name in the blank beside the statement. Please use each persons name only once.

_____ Has had their neck muscles tighten.

_____ Has been unable to concentrate.

_____ Has had a hard time falling asleep.

_____ Has felt the need to exercise more.

_____ Does not eat any junk food.

_____ Has never missed a day of school.

_____ Has had "butterflies" in their stomach.

_____ Has gone on a diet to lose weight.

_____ Has been too busy to eat properly.

_____ Has felt too tired and worn out to keep going.

_____ Has stayed up really late to study for a test.

_____ Has gone on a diet to gain weight.

CLASSROOM PUZZLE

WHAT'S THE POINT?

◉ **To help each student recognize his importance to the group.** It is important that each class member recognize his importance to the group. This activity illustrates visually how each individual is necessary to complete the picture.

DESCRIPTION OF THE TECHNIQUE:

◉ Cut a large piece of white tag board like a puzzle with enough pieces for every person in the room.

◉ Ask each person to draw their likeness on a puzzle piece.

◉ Fasten or glue the pieces together.

◉ Display in the classroom.

◉ Use as a focus for class discussions on unity, friendship, personal contributions, interdependence, etc.

◉ Variations
  • Have students design their own individual puzzles. Thoughts for each piece include what makes me me, my strengths, my family, my moods, my feelings, etc.
  • Students can draw, use pictures from magazines, use words, use symbols, etc.

PLEASE NOTE!

◉ When asking students to do individual puzzles, give them the choice to display or not display.

THOUGHTS...

_____
_____
_____
_____
_____
_____
_____
_____
_____
_____
_____
_____
_____

 INCLUSION  CONTROL  AFFECTION   COMPETENCY

✔✔   ✔

HELPING STUDENTS WITH
SPECIAL NEEDS FEEL WELCOME
There Is No Perfect Class

 WHAT'S THE POINT?

◎ **To make sure that students with special needs feel wanted and accepted by every-one.** With current mainstreaming objectives we all receive students with medical, mental or emotional difficulties. Most teachers and most kids have had little experience with special needs kids. Therefore it is important that we all work to make sure that these kids are accepted and understood.

 DESCRIPTION OF THE TECHNIQUE:

◎ **Build awareness in your classroom by teaching about the different types of special needs that people have.**

◎ **Some ideas include:**
  - Outside resource speakers.
  - Role playing as with crutches, wheelchairs, blindfolds, etc.
  - Books about people with special needs or disabilities.
  - Videos or films.

◎ **Welcome the special needs student just as you do every other student.** Don't over react or under react or your other students will do likewise.

◎ **Ask the special needs student if he or she wants their condition shared with the rest of the class before doing it.**

◎ **Ask the special needs student what you or the students might do to make their life better in the classroom.** Never assume that you know what's best for them.

◎ **Get the special needs student with a partner and with small groups right away.** Don't leave them sitting isolated and alone.

◎ **If a student suddenly disappears as in the case of accidents, illnesses or surgery, discuss the disappearance honestly with the class.** If the student will return with special needs, contact the student before hand and ask him or her what they would like the class to know about their returning.

 PLEASE NOTE!

◎ **What we understand we do not fear, and when we don't fear we are able to address differences in supporting ways.**

 INCLUSION CONTROL AFFECTION  COMPETENCY

✓   ✓✓

WELCOMING NEW STUDENTS

 WHAT'S THE POINT?

⑥ To help students new to the school fit into the routine and develop friendships.

 DESCRIPTION OF THE TECHNIQUE:

⑥ The following are ideas that have been used successfully in many schools.

⑥ **Interviewing**
New students are interviewed by a current student. The results of the interview are posted on a central bulletin board (see sample sheets on the next pages), written up in the school paper, shown on the school TV station, broadcast over the school radio, or announced over the school PA system. You might want to check for permission with the student or the students parents before doing some of the above, especially if the information is going outside the school.

⑥ **Buddy System**
A student knowledgeable about the functioning of the school is assigned to the student. They take the new student on a tour of the school, introduce them to the teachers and other students, and in general help them understand what's happening and help them get started.

⑥ **Welcoming Bag**
A bag made of paper, plastic, or canvas or a folder, all printed with the school logo, is handed to the student. This contains all the information the student needs to take home. Some schools include pencils with the school name, crayons, paper for the first day, bumper stickers, or anything that they can identify with the school. These can be prepared in advance. They save hunting through stacks of papers for the forms while the parents and new student wait anxiously in the office. They also make it easier for parent or student to get all the vital papers home.

⑥ **Introducing The School Using Video**
New students and their parents are shown a video that introduces them to many aspects of the school. These are usually made by students using students. They can include any variety of ideas. Some possibilities are a tour of the building, special programs like band and music, expectations for behavior in halls, cafeteria, and assemblies, words of welcome from the principal and some of the teachers, and comments from students on how things really are.

continued on next page

 INCLUSION  CONTROL  AFFECTION COMPETENCY

◎ **Welcoming People**

This is by far the most important. All people who come in contact with the new student and the parents act like they are glad to see them. Enrolling the new student becomes top priority in the office. The receiving teacher(s) welcome the student to class **no matter what**. Statements like "I got the last two students." or "My section is full." are saved for private conversations with the principal later in the day.

PLEASE NOTE!

◎ **The first few minutes or hours are perhaps the most important in the career of a student in your school.** The impressions gained and the behavior encountered in those early moments can set the tone for the attitude of the student and the parents and many of the later interactions for as long as the family stays with you.

THOUGHTS...

_____
_____
_____
_____
_____
_____
_____
_____
_____
_____
_____
_____
_____
_____
_____
_____
_____
_____
_____
_____
_____
_____
_____
_____
_____
_____
_____
_____
_____
_____
_____
_____
_____

WELCOME

(paste picture)

Name _____

Advisor _____ Grade _____

Came from _____

Favorite music group _____

Favorite things to do _____

Favorite foods _____

Sports _____

What likes best about new school _____

What misses most about old school _____

I'M HERE!!

(paste picture)

Name _____

Teacher _____ Grade _____

Came from _____

Favorite color _____ Favorite food _____

Brothers or sisters _____

Pets _____ Likes to _____

What likes best about new school _____

What misses most about old school _____

 INCLUSION  CONTROL AFFECTION COMPETENCY

✓✓   ✓   ✓

CLASS MEETINGS

 WHAT'S THE POINT?

⑥ To provide a setting that provides structure and opportunity for the entire class to meet together and to address individual and group concerns.

 DESCRIPTION OF THE TECHNIQUE:

⑥ Determine a regular time (weekly or more often) for students to meet as a group.

⑥ **Establish the physical format with your students.** It works best when students form a circle, either with their chairs or by sitting on the floor.

⑥ **Determine the agenda prior to each meeting.** This can be done by a suggestion box, a posted agenda for students and the teacher to list topics, or an "emergency" meeting to deal with a sudden problem that affects one or more of the students.

⑥ **Establish the discussion parameters.** Some suggestions are:
  • Only one person at a time will talk.
  • Hand out two cards. As each student takes a turn the card is thrown into the center of the circle. Once the student's cards are gone he or she may not speak again.
  • There will be no "put downs."
  • Students may choose to speak or not speak.
  • A designated student or adult can act as a monitor to keep the meeting focused, especially when beginning this technique.
  • A timekeeper will keep tract of the time and signal 5 minutes left, 2 minutes left, meeting over.

⑥ **Variation**
Students number off. Even numbers place their chairs in an inner circle. Odd numbers place their chairs in the outer circle. The topic of the day is discussed by the student sitting in front with their partner, meaning the student sitting behind them. After a specified amount of time the topic is them discussed by only the inner circle. It is the responsibility of those in the inner circle to make sure they only express their partners's viewpoint After a specified time the partners change chairs, and for the second half of the meeting the new inner circle members share the ideas of their partners. Some follow up discussion on how they felt about the process and whether their ideas were clearly shared by their partner is helpful before ending the meeting.

⑥ **Variation**
Using a ball of string students make a statement and throw the ball to another circle member. This will form a web (see **BUILDING THE WEB**). It is possible to do a double web if the discussion continues.

continued on next page

@ **Variation**

Before the meeting begins have two or more students develop a short skit which illustrates a concern. Have them act it out in the circle, and let students discuss possible solutions.

@ **Variation**

Use the meeting as a compliment time. As the students go around the circle each speaker will give a compliment to a classmate.

THOUGHTS...

_____
_____
_____
_____
_____
_____
_____
_____
_____
_____
_____
_____
_____
_____
_____
_____
_____
_____
_____
_____
_____
_____
_____
_____
_____
_____
_____
_____
_____
_____
_____
_____
_____
_____
_____
_____
_____
_____

 INCLUSION CONTROL AFFECTION COMPETENCY

✓✓   ✓

FORMING CLASSROOM GROUPS

 WHAT'S THE POINT?

⑤ **To establish working groups in the classroom.** Working in groups can be an integral part of a well-functioning classroom if formed in a manner that promotes optimal learning and cooperation.

 DESCRIPTION OF THE TECHNIQUE:

⑤ Here are some ideas for group forming in use around the country.
⑤ **Some of the time teachers let students form their own groups.** They may only set a limit such as size (3 to 5 in a group).
⑤ **Some of the time teachers have kids count off.** This makes it strictly arbitrary and cuts down on arguing.
⑤ **Some of the time teachers pick group leaders or captains and allow them to select their group members.** This can be a little hard on the low self esteem students.
⑤ **Some of the time teachers select the group members.** Some thoughts to keep in mind when selecting:
  • Leaders distributed evenly.
  • Boy/girl ratio even.
  • Various academic levels included.
  • All same academic level for skill development.
  • Shy, popular, aggressive students evenly distributed.
  • Students have a friend in their group.
  • Students don't have a friend so they're forced to make new ones.

 PLEASE NOTE!

⑤ **When people (students or adults) are assigned to groups they almost always feel that every other group is better than theirs.** In other words the grass is always greener.

⑤ **Variety is the key.** Sometimes you choose, sometimes they choose. Short term is the word. Rotate or reselect groups periodically.

THOUGHTS...

_____
_____
_____
_____
_____
_____
_____
_____

CHAPTER 9

WINNING WAYS

for

CONTROL

 INCLUSION CONTROL AFFECTION COMPETENCY

✓   ✓   ✓   ✓

MODEL, MODEL, MODEL
Do As I Do

 WHAT'S THE POINT?

⑥ **To model on a daily basis the behaviors I want to see in the kids in front of me.**
Teachers who model the behaviors they want, such as being courteous, respecting others, and remaining in control of themselves tend to have classes that exhibit the same behaviors.

 DESCRIPTION OF THE TECHNIQUE:

⑥ **Simply show your students through your own behavior how to act in the classroom. Some examples are:**
- Talking in a quiet voice.
- Listening to others.
- Being helpful to others.
- Treating students with respect, regardless of behavior.
- Making eye contact.
- Smiling.
- Keeping personal materials neat and tidy.
- Respecting others' property.
- Treating every student like they're your best friend.
- Leading with empathy.
- Using the problem solving model.
- Showing an interest in every student.
- Using "can do" messages instead of "can't do" messages.

PLEASE NOTE!

⑥ **Modeling is the most powerful behavior you can use in the classroom. Students do as we do, not as we say.** So save your breath and start doing.

 THOUGHTS...

_____
_____
_____
_____
_____
_____
_____
_____
_____
_____
_____

THE PROBLEM SOLVING MODEL

 WHAT'S THE POINT?

⌬ **To implement THE PROBLEM SOLVING MODEL throughout the entire school.** A cooperative, nonviolent way to solve problems is a learned behavior and must be taught. This is a model that can be used by students, teachers and the class as a whole to handle almost any problem that comes up.

 DESCRIPTION OF THE TECHNIQUE:

⌬ **Step 1. Empathy**

"Really upset, huh?"

"Bet you're feeling…?"

"If that had happened to me I would be feeling…?

⌬ **Step 2. Offer Choices**

"Would you rather pay for this or wash and wax both cars this weekend."

NOW GO TO STEP 6 OR…

⌬ **Step 3. Sincere Question**

"What do you plan to do about this?"

"How do you plan to handle this?"

⌬ **Step 4. Permission to Share**

"Would you like to hear what others have tried?"

"I have some thoughts on that. Would you like to hear them?"

⌬ **Step 5. Share Possibilities**

"Some kids…?"

⌬ **Step 6. Examine Consequences**

"How will this work for you?"

⌬ **Step 7. Endings**

   a) Allow to Solve or Not

"Good luck! Let me know how it goes."

   b) Use "Feel free to…"

"Feel free to eat in the cafeteria again when the mess is taken care of."

   c) Take ownership

"I have some ideas on solving that. Most kids like their own ideas best. However, if you don't have any ideas by 2:30 pm, we will go with mine."

continued on next page

⑥ **Think through how the wording might be changed to fit the grade level of your students** (see the following pages for some school examples). The best way to create these models is to do so with the students.

⑥ **Remember the more you get the wording from the students, the more you up the odds for the model having meaning.**

⑥ **Present the modified model to the students.** Teach the model through discussion and role playing using student and whole class examples.

⑥ **Post the model in your Problem Solving Place (see SENDING KIDS TO THE PROBLEM SOLVING PLACE) and in a place that can be see by the whole class.**

⑥ **Use this model whenever disputes arise between any members of the student body.**

⑥ **Use THE PROBLEM SOLVING WORKSHEET** (see following page) **as you work with students.** The form can then be filed in the students folder as the permanent record of the conference.

 PLEASE NOTE!

⑥ **To be effective regardless of the format finally agreed upon, the PROBLEM SOLVING MODEL needs to be used by as many people as possible and in as many situations as possible in the classroom and in the school.**

THOUGHTS…

_____
_____
_____
_____
_____
_____
_____
_____
_____
_____
_____
_____
_____
_____
_____
_____
_____

Based on the Problem Solving Model developed by Jim Fay and Foster W. Cline, M.D. of the Cline/Fay Love and Logic Institute, Inc., Golden, CO. Contact them for materials or speaking at 1-800-455-7557.

THE PROBLEM SOLVING MODEL WORKSHEET

This form can be used as you conference with a student and then filed as a record of the conference.

Student _____ **Date** _____

Problem _____

_____

_____

Empathy _____

_____

Choices Offered _____

_____

_____

_____

_____

NOW GO TO EXAMINE CONSEQUENCES OR...

The Sincere Question _____

_____

Permission to Share _____

_____

_____

Possibilities or Options _____

_____

_____

_____

_____

Examine Consequences _____

_____

_____

_____

_____

_____

End the Conversation

1. Allow to solve or not _____

_____

_____

_____

2. Use "Feel free to…" _____

_____

_____

_____

3. Take ownership _____

_____

_____

_____

NOTES:

_____

_____

_____

_____

Based on the Problem Solving Model developed by Jim Fay and Foster W. Cline, M.D. of the Cline/Fay Love and Logic Institute, Inc., Golden, CO.   Contact them for materials or speaking at 1-800-455-7557.

THE PROBLEM SOLVING MODEL
An Elementary School Example

1. Each person tell what happened.

2. Each person say how they feel.

3. Each person say what they are willing to do to solve the problem.

4. Agree on one solution.

5. Shake hands.

6. Let the teacher know the problem is taken care of.

THE PROBLEM SOLVING MODEL
A Middle School/ High School Example

1. Describe to each other what happened.

2. Tell each other how you feel.

3. Make a list of two or more ways to handle the problem.

4. Talk about how each way might or might not work.

5. Agree on one.

6. Allow each person to restate the agreement.

7. Let the adult in charge know the problem has been handled.

FORMS FOR PROBLEM SOLVING
Sheets for Students To Use When They Have Created A Problem

WHAT'S THE POINT?

◎ **To use a written activity to help students work through owning and solving the problem they have just created.**

DESCRIPTION OF THE TECHNIQUE:

◎ **Most adults solve their problems by first talking it out.** Very few of us have a problem, grab a form, and sit down and fill it out. The same is true with kids. However let's get real. While it is always best to talk students through the problem solving process, sometimes it just isn't possible. There are days when you have too many problems and too little time. Sometimes the problem is just minor and you've discussed it a million times. Sometimes after you and the student(s) have talked through the problem, it helps the students cement the ideas by writing down what was just agreed upon. If any of these situations turn up in your classroom you might want to use one of the forms on the following pages, or work with your students to develop one of your own.

PLEASE NOTE!

◎ **If a student has problems writing, using these activity sheets becomes a punishment and defeats the whole purpose.** These sheets are also not something to be criticized and marked for spelling, punctuation and grammar.

THOUGHTS...

_____
_____
_____
_____
_____
_____
_____
_____
_____
_____
_____
_____
_____
_____
_____
_____
_____
_____

 **HERE'S WHAT HAPPENED:**

 **HERE'S WHAT I WOULD DO NEXT TIME:**

WHAT HAPPENED?
HOW COULD YOU SOLVE IT?

Name _____ Date _____

What were you trying to do? _____
_____
_____
_____

What happened? _____
_____
_____
_____

What caused it to happen? _____
_____
_____
_____

How do you feel about what happened? _____
_____
_____
_____

How do you plan to solve the problem? _____
_____
_____
_____

How can you use what you learned to solve problems in the future? _____
_____
_____
_____

PROBLEM SOLVING SHEET

Name _____ Date _____

Here's my problem _____
_____
_____
_____

Here's how I handled it _____
_____
_____
_____

Here's how it worked out _____
_____
_____
_____

Here's how I would handle it next time _____
_____
_____
_____

Here's what I learned _____
_____
_____
_____

PROBLEM OWNERSHIP STATEMENTS
Teaching Yourself and Others The 1-2-3 Step Problem Ownership Statement

WHAT'S THE POINT?

🌀 **To develop in yourself and in your students the skill of owning one's own problems.** This is really a fairly easy way to teach those all powerful "I messages."

DESCRIPTION OF THE TECHNIQUE:

🌀 Practice with your own problems and then teach your students the following sequence:

🌀 **When the problem is mine:**
- **Step 1. I will say how I feel.**
  - I am upset about…
  - I feel angry when…
  - I am feeling disappointed that…
- **Step 2. I will describe the problem from my point of view.**
  - You call me names in class.
  - The homework isn't coming in.
  - You are constantly out of your seat.
- **Step 3. I will state how the problem directly affects me.**
  - Because I don't feel I deserve it.
  - Because I don't feel I am helping you learn all you can.
  - Because I don't want to have to ask you to leave the room.

🌀 **It the other person says, "Who cares." or something equally obnoxious, I will simply say "I just wanted to let you know how I feel."** Then I will break eye contact and walk away.

🌀 I will allow the other person time to think over what I have said.

🌀 **If the behavior does not self correct I can either:**
- Let it go.
- Engage the person in problem solving (see **THE PROBLEM SOLVING MODEL**).

🌀 **Variation**
With younger students, ages 4 through 6 or so, use only the first two steps. It is important even at this young age to teach the follow up "I just wanted you to know how I felt." and walk away part. Many people, when confronted with an "I message" feel embarrassed and initially get defensive. They need thinking time before they can take action.

continued on next page

⑥ **Variation**

When students are having problems with others, have them write out their Problem Ownership Statement first, then say it to the other person (see the following page for the **OWNING MY PROBLEM** worksheet).

THOUGHTS...

OWNING MY PROBLEM

I feel *(how I feel)* _____

when *(the problem as I see it)* _____

_____

because *(how the problem affects me)* _____

_____ .

If the other person says "So!" or "Who cares!" or some thing else not helpful, I will say

_____

_____

and then I will _____ .

If the other person says "I'm sorry, I didn't mean to upset you." or something helpful, I will

say _____

_____

and then I will _____ .

Signed _____ Dated _____

SENDING KIDS TO A PROBLEM SOLVING PLACE
A Place for Individuals, Twosomes, and Small Groups

WHAT'S THE POINT?

⚙ **To provide students with the opportunity to solve their disputes in a private setting.** The truth is that the only people who can solve a problem are the people who are involved in the problem. We must have the courage to let go and allow them to learn to solve their own disputes by being allowed to solve their own disputes.

DESCRIPTION OF THE TECHNIQUE:

⚙ **Work with the class to develop a problem solving model** (see **THE PROBLEM SOLVING MODEL** for ideas and samples).

⚙ **Select a place that is relatively private to be the Problem Solving Place.** Some examples:
   • Pre-K and Kindergarten - a bench in the room designated the Peace Bench.
   • Elementary School - a table called the Talk It Over Table or the Problem Solving Table.
   • Elementary School - a carpeted area with some cushions called the Peace Rug or the Pow Wow Rug.
   • Junior High/High School - a Problem Solving Room. These are usually staffed with an adult who is trained to either lead the students through the process or to be available to the students working through the problem on their own.

⚙ **Post the Problem Solving Steps in the Problem Solving Place.**

⚙ **When conflict arises separate students and give them time to cool down.**

⚙ **Then ask the students if they want to go the the Problem Solving Place, or if they want to wait until you can be part of the process.**

⚙ **Ask students to let you know when the problem is resolved.** Control yourself! You do not need to know all the gory details. You just need to know if it is resolved, yes, or no.

⚙ **If it is resolved say "Thanks for solving the problem."**

⚙ **If it is not resolved ask, "Do you need more time, or do you need me to sit in?"**

PLEASE NOTE!

⚙ **It works best if students are allowed to cool down and be in the "thinking state" before going to the Problem Solving Place.** It also works best if you offer the Problem Solving Place as a choice. Ordering kids to solve a problem "or else" is doomed to failure.

continued on next page

🌀 **Having kids fill out a problem solving sheet before the problem is talked through is also not effective.** First, if the kid has problems with reading and writing the exercise becomes punitive. Second, we as adults rarely write out our problems, we talk them out. Why do we think students operate differently?

🌀 **What about kids who refuse to work on the problem?** Just say, "No problem. Let me know when you're ready to talk about it." Students should be kept from regular classroom activities until the problem is taken care of. No rush.

THOUGHTS...

_____
_____
_____
_____
_____
_____
_____
_____
_____
_____
_____
_____
_____
_____
_____
_____
_____
_____
_____
_____
_____
_____
_____
_____
_____
_____
_____
_____
_____
_____
_____
_____
_____
_____
_____
_____
_____

STUDENT DIRECTED PARENT CONFERENCES

WHAT'S THE POINT?

🌀 **To hold students responsible for conducting the parent/teacher/student conferences.** We are going to ask students to analyze their own progress, develop their own plans for improvement, and relate this information to their parents in person. If you want to see improvement in academics and behavior, it is necessary to get kids involved in this process.

DESCRIPTION OF THE TECHNIQUE:

🌀 **Fill out report cards as usual.** Bummer, you thought you were going to get out of this step.

🌀 **Round up a lot of engaging work for your class.** Anything you think will keep them involved while you conference one-on-one.

🌀 **With report card and STUDENT DIRECTED PARENT CONFERENCE SHEET** (see following page) **in front of you, call students one-by-one to a private spot in the room for conferencing.**

🌀 **Ask the questions on the STUDENT DIRECTED PARENT CONFERENCE SHEET.**

🌀 **Record the answers.**

🌀 **Schedule the parent conference.** Sit back and let the student do the talking.

🌀 **Every time a parent asks a question, refer the question to the student.**

PLEASE NOTE!

🌀 **A word to the wise.** Keep brothers, sisters, distant relatives, family, friends, and neighbors outside.

🌀 **Anything that cannot be said in front of the student probably does not need to be discussed between parent and teacher.** There are very few exceptions.

THOUGHTS...

_____
_____
_____
_____
_____
_____
_____
_____
_____
_____
_____
_____
_____
_____

STUDENT DIRECTED
PARENT CONFERENCE WORKSHEET

1. What about this report card do you feel good about?_____

   _____

   _____

   _____

   _____

2. What areas of this report card show need for improvement?_____

   _____

   _____

   _____

   _____

3. What are your plans for bringing about change in the areas in need of improvement?

   _____

   _____

   _____

   _____

4. Other: _____

   _____

   _____

   _____

   _____

PHONE CONFERENCING
The Parent Calls You

 WHAT'S THE POINT?

⑥ **To communicate with the parent by phone.** The more the student is involved in the process, the more you can expect to see a behavioral change.

 DESCRIPTION OF THE TECHNIQUE:

⑥ **The Parent Calls You**
- Shift into neutral. Going on the defensive will not help.
- Apologize (if appropriate).
- Ask the parent to help you understand. Listen! Listen! Listen!
- Empathize.
- Take responsibility for the current situation.
- Offer alternatives or options.
- Come to some agreement.
- Ask for their thoughts and/or feelings.

 PLEASE NOTE!

⑥ **Here you have little opportunity to involve the student.**

⑥ **Variation**
Request that the parent call you back when the child is available to be part of the conversation.

⑥ **Variation**
Ask the parent for permission to put the student on the speaker phone for a three-way discussion

THOUGHTS...

_____
_____
_____
_____
_____
_____
_____
_____
_____
_____
_____

SHARING BY PHONE
You Call the Parent

WHAT'S THE POINT?

⑥ **To communicate with the parent by phone.** The more the student is involved in the process, the more you can expect to see a behavioral change.

DESCRIPTION OF THE TECHNIQUE:

⑥ **You Call the Parents**
- Identify yourself.
  - "I'm June Selby, Brad's teacher."
- Ask permission to share.
  - "Do you have a minute, I'd like to talk with you about something that happened with Brad today?"
- Describe what happened.
  - Discuss the incident objectively. Drop emotionalizing, moralizing and judging.
- Share how you and/or the student have planned to handle this. (see **THE PROBLEM SOLVING MODEL**).
- End with "Does this sound workable to you?" or "What are your thoughts and feelings?"

PLEASE NOTE!

⑥ **This works best if you offer calling the parents as a choice to the student**, as in "Do you think you and I can work this out, or do you think we need to involve your parents?" If you don't want to offer this as a choice, at least let the student know that you plan to call as in "I just wanted to let you know that I will be talking with your parents tonight."

⑥ **Variation**
Have the student present when you call. After concluding the conversation ask the parent if he/she would like to talk to the student. Be prepared to hand the phone to the student if the parent requests, preferably at the end of the conversation.

⑥ **Variation**
Have the student make the phone call to the parent. This works best if you and the student discuss what is to be said first. It also helps if the student is one you can trust not to "go dramatic" on you when handed the phone.

PLEASE NOTE!

⑥ **Be prepared to pass an unhappy caller on to a higher authority.** Use the "swear stopper" when necessary. For example, "Excuse me. I can handle the problem, but not the swearing." Never, never, never argue, make excuses, or defend.

Based on the *Problem Solving Model* developed by Jim Fay and Foster W. Cline, M.D. of the Cline/Fay Love and Logic Institute, Inc., Golden, CO. Contact them for materials and speaking at 1-800-455-7557.

WHAT SETS ME OFF?
Things That Trigger Anger

WHAT'S THE POINT?

🌀 To make students aware of situations that trigger their inappropriate behavior.

DESCRIPTION OF THE TECHNIQUE:

🌀 Spend time in a class meeting or during instructional time discussing what others do or say that leads them into inappropriate behavior or as they say, "sets me off." Talk about what people in different groups do:
- What do their parents do?
- What their friends do?
- What do their teachers do?
- What do _____ do?
- Have each student fill out **WHAT SETS ME OFF** (see following worksheet).
- During follow-up lessons have students talk about things they could do instead of getting mad when somebody uses a "set me off" behavior on them.

🌀 Some suggestions for grouping are:
- Randomly group
- Students with like triggers group
- Whole class discussion

🌀 Refer to other **WINNING WAYS** in this book for ideas on teaching alternative behaviors to getting mad.

THOUGHTS...

_____

_____

_____

_____

_____

_____

_____

_____

_____

_____

_____

WHAT SETS ME OFF?
Worksheet

List in the appropriate column the things others
do that upset you enough that you change your behavior.

FRIENDS	TEACHERS	PARENTS	OTHERS

ALTERNATIVES TO FIGHT OR FLIGHT
Teaching Students Approaches To Handling Minor Problems

 WHAT'S THE POINT?

⑥ To teach students alternative behaviors to fight or flight that they can use when they encounter minor problems on the playground, in the school, in the neighborhood, or in their homes.

 DESCRIPTION OF THE TECHNIQUE:

⑥ **Discuss the fight or flight concept.** Some students fight when they have a problem and some students run away. Talk about how each of these approaches might work out for them. "What happens when you fight at home, in school, etc.?"

⑥ **Brainstorm a list of problems they encounter on a daily basis.** List on the board, overhead, or flip chart. Discuss what might happen and how they might feel if they fought or ran away from each of these situations.

⑥ **Now teach by modeling and role playing alternative ways to handle these problems.** Some ideas to include are:
- **Talk It Out** (see **THE PROBLEM SOLVING MODEL**)
- **Use "I feel" messages**
  - "I feel mad when you take my truck."
  - If the other person says "Sorry" say "Thanks."
  - If the other person says "So" just say "I just wanted you to know how I feel," and walk away.
- **Take 10**
  - Say "I'm too mad to talk now."
  - Walk away until you calm down and can choose a problem solving approach to use.
- **Use Humor**
  - Kid says, "You're stupid."
  - Say, 'That's the funniest thing I have heard today."
  - Smile and walk away.
- **Say Stop**
  - Put your hand out, palm up and out.
  - Firmly say, "Stop."
  - Turn and walk away.
- **Walk Away**
  - Ignore what the person says or does.
  - Turn your back and calmly walk away.
  - Don't go back no matter what they say or do.
  - Just keep walking.

continued on next page

- **Agree and Restate**
  - Kid says, "You're stupid."
  - Say, "That's one way of thinking. I think I am pretty smart."
  - Then walk away.
- **Ask for Help**
  - Find the nearest adult.
  - Say "I need help with a problem."
  - Ask "Would you help me with my problem?"

⊚ **Make or have students make posters of these approaches.**

⊚ **Model these approaches as you interact with the students.**

⊚ **When students use fight or flight, allow them to cool down.** Then ask them which one of these approaches they would be willing to use to handle the problem.

⊚ **Guide students through the steps.**

⊚ **Reteach these approaches as needed.**

 PLEASE NOTE!

⊚ **The idea is to help students understand that they have the power and the skills they need to own and solve their own minor problems.** It is also important to help them understand that some problems are major, and that asking for help is sometimes the wisest thing to do. Also really stress that when they feel frightened or in danger, go immediately to an adult for help.

THOUGHTS...

_____
_____
_____
_____
_____
_____
_____
_____
_____
_____
_____
_____
_____
_____
_____
_____
_____
_____

 INCLUSION  CONTROL  AFFECTION  COMPETENCY

WHAT DO I DO NOW?
Eight Steps To Resolution

 WHAT'S THE POINT?

🌀 **To develop a plan for working with those very difficult students.** As you know, when dealing with these kids, flitting from technique to technique or operating off the top of your head is an exercise in futility.

 DESCRIPTION OF THE TECHNIQUE:

- Select a quiet time with no students present. You might want to ask a colleague to come in and work with you.
- Place a copy of the **EIGHT STEPS TO RESOLUTION** worksheet in front of you (see following page).
- Work through the worksheet step by step, being as honest and realistic as possible. This is not a wish list, this is an "I can really do this" plan.
- Review the plan and get input and support from any or all of the following: parents, supervisors, the student.
- Implement the plan.

THOUGHTS...

_____
_____
_____
_____
_____
_____
_____
_____
_____
_____
_____
_____
_____
_____
_____
_____

EIGHT STEPS TO RESOLUTION

Student _____

Teacher _____

Date _____

WHAT DO I DO NOW?

Step 1: Describe the student's observable behavior(s).
Describe without emotion or judgment the behavior(s) you would like to see eliminated or decreased. Select no more than 2 or 3.

1. _____
2. _____
3. _____

Step 2: Ask the basic questions.
Can I teach the rest of the class with this behavior - yes or no?
Can other students in the class learn with this behavior - yes or no?

Step 3: Examine the relationship.
Am I working on relationship building? Refer to **Prevention Strategies** (see following pages) and list those not in place.

1. _____
2. _____
3. _____
4. _____

Step 4: Look closely at the curriculum.
Can the student do the work assigned successfully 70 to 80% of the time if he tries? If yes go on to Step 5. If not, what changes might I consider making? After deciding what is possible, remember to involve the student in the final decision making.

1. _____
2. _____
3. _____
4. _____

Step 5: Describe what I can't control.
Make a list. Be specific and honest.

1. _____
2. _____
3. _____
4. _____

Step 6: Describe what I can control.

Make a list. Be specific and honest.

1. _____
2. _____
3. _____

Step 7: List the Intervention Strategies.

Refer to the following pages for **Intervention Strategies**. Select some you think might work and that you are willing to experiment with in this case. Referral to Special Ed. might be a consideration.

1. _____
2. _____
3. _____
4. _____

Step 8: Make the plan and follow the plan.

Remember both **Prevention Strategies** (including curriculum and special education concerns) and **Intervention Strategies**. Narrow the students options until resolution.

Opening Plan

(The first strategy I will try.)

_____
_____

Options Narrowed

(If the above doesn't work, I will try this.)

_____
_____

Options Narrowed

(If the above doesn't work, I will now try this.)

_____
_____

Bottom Line

(The point at which the student needs to be referred to the administration for testing, suspension, expulsion, or outside placement.)

_____
_____
_____
_____

EIGHT STEPS TO RESOLUTION
My Master Plan

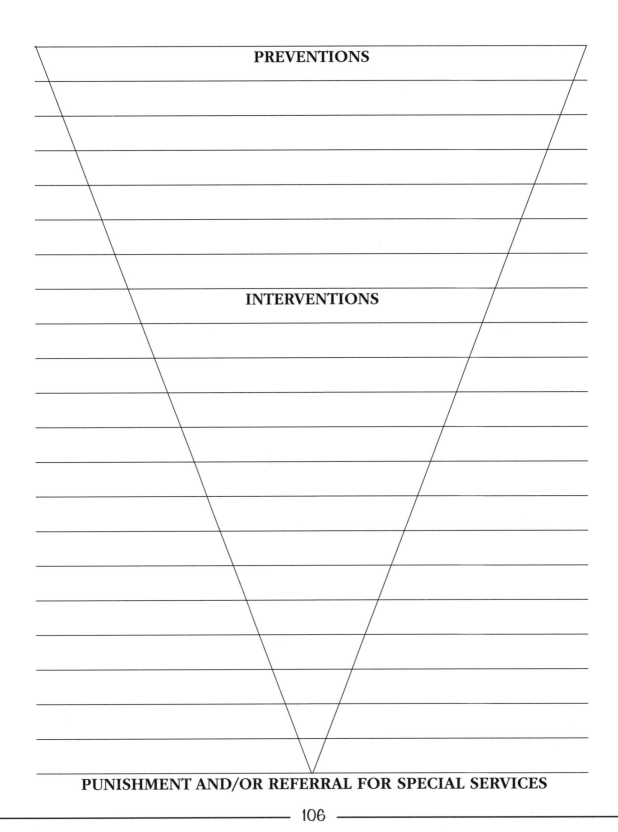

PREVENTIONS

INTERVENTIONS

PUNISHMENT AND/OR REFERRAL FOR SPECIAL SERVICES

 INCLUSION CONTROL AFFECTION COMPETENCY

✔   ✔✔

STARTING THE SCHOOL YEAR RIGHT
Policies and Procedures

 WHAT'S THE POINT?

◉ To insure that the teacher has a clearly defined set of policies and procedures about how the class is to be run <u>before</u> the students arrive, and then <u>actively teaches</u> these policies and procedures to the students. Failing to plan is planning to fail. So make your plan and follow it to success.

 DESCRIPTION OF THE TECHNIQUE:

◉ Teachers sit down alone or with colleagues before school starts and complete the **POLICIES AND PROCEDURES PLANNING SHEETS (see following pages).**

◉ During the bonding period (the first few periods or days of the class) the teacher **actively teaches all policies and procedures.** Actively teaches means that the teacher demonstrates and the class practices. It does not mean assuming students know what the teacher wants or handing out a typed sheet and saying, "Read this and do what it says."

◉ The policies and procedures are retaught as needed.

◉ Some classrooms reteach the beginning of each nine week period.

◉ Some classrooms reteach the beginning of each semester.

◉ Some classrooms make videos of the more important procedures and have them available for new students to view and misbehaving students to review.

 PLEASE NOTE!

◉ **The following CLASSROOM POLICIES AND PROCEDURES PLANNING SHEET is a model.** Please feel free to redo and make it fit your situation. The idea is to think through or anticipate as much as possible everything that is going to take place and then be prepared with a plan to handle it. Trying to make decisions off the top of our heads while surrounded by 25 or more students does not work too well for most of us.

CLASSROOM POLICIES AND PROCEDURES

Area	Plan for Handling	Tc Tell Assume
BEGINNING THE CLASS		
1. Entering class	_____	_____
2. Coming to order	_____	_____
3. Opening activity	_____	_____
4. Attendance	_____	_____
5. Lunch count	_____	_____
6. Collections	_____	_____
7. Class rules	_____	_____
8. _____	_____	_____
ENDING THE CLASS		
1. Room clean up	_____	_____
2. Closing activity	_____	_____
3. Announcements	_____	_____
4. Dismissal procedure	_____	_____
5. _____	_____	_____
CLASSROOM PROCEDURES		
1. Getting stu. attention	_____	_____
2. Stu. getting your attention	_____	_____
3. Materials/supplies	_____	_____
4. Sharpening pencils	_____	_____
5. Passing out things	_____	_____
6. Collecting things	_____	_____
7. Work done time	_____	_____
8. Coming late	_____	_____
9. Not bringing materials	_____	_____
10. Gum/candy/food	_____	_____

continued on next page

11. Coats/hats/clothes   _____   _____

12. Toys, beepers, etc.   _____   _____

13. Gang signs, etc.   _____   _____

14. _____   _____   _____

GROUP TIME

1. Forming groups   _____   _____

2. Out of group behavior   _____   _____

3. _____   _____   _____

CLASS WORK

1. Heading papers   _____   _____

2. Pen or pencil   _____   _____

3. Legibility/computer   _____   _____

4. Paper - front/back   _____   _____

5. Incomplete papers   _____   _____

6. Late papers   _____   _____

7. Missed work   _____   _____

8. No name papers   _____   _____

9. _____   _____   _____

HOMEWORK

1. Assigning   _____   _____

2. Late policy   _____   _____

3. Missed assignments   _____   _____

4. Collecting work   _____   _____

5. _____   _____   _____

SPECIAL EVENTS

1. Fire drill   _____   _____

2. Other drills   _____   _____

3. Intercom/phone   _____   _____

continued on next page

4. Room visitors   _____   _____

5. _____   _____   _____

OUTSIDE CLASSROOM

1. Assemblies   _____   _____

2. Playground   _____   _____

3. Lunch room   _____   _____

4. Halls   _____   _____

5. Before school   _____   _____

6. After school   _____   _____

7. Bathroom   _____   _____

8. Leaving the class   _____   _____

9. Field trips   _____   _____

10. Busses   _____   _____

11. _____   _____   _____

 INCLUSION  CONTROL  AFFECTION  COMPETENCY

MAKING THE RULES

 WHAT'S THE POINT?

⑤ **To involve students in making classroom rules.** Effective Schools' data suggests that when teachers take time in the fall to develop rules with students, classrooms function more effectively, disruptions are reduced, and students' learning time is increased.

DESCRIPTION OF THE TECHNIQUE:

- Be prepared with a couple rules. Say to the students, "These are the rules I need in order to teach."
- Ask students, " What rules do you need in order to learn?" Record every suggestion. You now have your class rules.
- If you feel the need to list consequences, try to avoid the step 1, step 2 approach. Instead just brainstorm a list of possibilities.
- Avoid material rewards and focus instead on generating ideas that are not material such as:
  - "When I do my work I'm learning lots."
  - "I feel good when I've learned something new."
  - "I'm one of the kids who's going to the next grade prepared."

- Periodically review the rules with the class. Ask the following questions:
  - Which rules are working for us?
  - Which rules don't we need anymore?
  - Are there any rules we can combine?
  - Are there any new rules we need to add?

- Middle school, high school, junior high school teachers. Sound too cumbersome to do with seven or eight classes? At least try the following:
  - State, "These are the rules I need to teach."
  - Ask, "Any thoughts, questions, or suggestions?"

- Some classrooms and schools operate under the "one rule" policy. The "one rule" is:

  In this school we do not cause a problem for ourselves or others.

- Concerned that you don't have enough rules to cover every misbehavior? Well not to worry. Remember your district has plenty. They need to because parents come with lawyers. So just remind kids that all classroom rules are superseded by district rules and regulations.

 THOUGHTS...

_____

_____

_____

_____

 INCLUSION CONTROL  AFFECTION  COMPETENCY

✓✓ ✓

NO NAME PAPERS
Papers With No Names

 WHAT'S THE POINT?

⑥ To handle the problem of papers with no names in a respectful manner, while holding the student responsible for the problem.

 DESCRIPTION OF THE TECHNIQUE:

⑥ Take a box, a basket, or some shelf space and label it the "No Name Paper Place."

⑥ When you get a paper with no name, put it in the "No Name Paper Place."

⑥ When students say "I handed in my paper and didn't get it back," reply "Why don't you look in the "No Name Paper Place?"

 PLEASE NOTE!

⑥ **We all forget from time to time.** Embarrassing the student will only insure resentment, not compliance.

THOUGHTS...

_____
_____
_____
_____
_____
_____
_____
_____
_____
_____
_____
_____
_____
_____
_____
_____
_____
_____
_____

LINING UP
Why Do We Have To?

WHAT'S THE POINT?

ⓖ To help students understand the need for lining up and participate in determining when it is necessary and when it isn't.

DESCRIPTION OF THE TECHNIQUE:

ⓖ **Have a class discussion about the need for lining up.**

ⓖ **Make a list of times during the school day when using lines might be needed.** Examples might be getting your food in the cafeteria, during fire drills, and using the water fountains.

ⓖ **Teach line behavior.** Have students role play appropriate behaviors for standing and moving in lines.

ⓖ **Then determine your policy and follow through.** Here are some examples of ways teachers around the country have successfully dealt with lining up:
- Some teachers let students determine the best way to move quickly, quietly, and safely to their destination (group or line).
- If the method selected is not working well, some teachers let students discuss it during a class meeting.
- Some teachers are comfortable only if students line up. To get student involvement they let the students develop line jobs such as line supervisor, middle line supervisor, and end of the line supervisor.

PLEASE NOTE!

ⓖ **Though lining up often creates problems such as power struggles, control issues, physical aggression, and complaining about fairness, there are times when it is critical that students line up with no questions asked.** Getting students involved in the process tends to eliminate some of these problems. And you middle school and high school people, don't think lining up isn't a problem for you. An emergency evacuation is no time for students to be running amok regardless of their age.

THOUGHTS...

_____
_____
_____
_____
_____
_____
_____
_____

 INCLUSION CONTROL  AFFECTION  COMPETENCY

HANDLING TARDIES
A Positive Approach

WHAT'S THE POINT?

⚙ To hold students responsible for being late in a way that says, "I'm glad to see you."

DESCRIPTION OF THE TECHNIQUE:

⚙ **As part of your regular classroom procedures, teach students what to do when they enter late.** Below is a process that has been successful in developing responsibility and reducing tardies in hundreds of classrooms.
  - No matter what time a student enters the room, make eye contact and smile.
  - Teach the following process:
    - Enter quietly, hang up gear if appropriate, go to seat and prepare to get started.
    - If you've missed lunch count take care of it at a time designated by the teacher.
    - If you're on the absentee list, take care of that using a process laid out by the teacher.
    - Quietly ask a responsible student what you have missed and what you need to be doing.

⚙ **Once the process is taught all you will need to do for the rest of the year is ask the question, "What do you need to do to get started?"**

PLEASE NOTE!

⚙ **What makes you want to get someplace on time?** Knowing you're going to be welcomed even if you're late, or knowing you're going to get bawled out?

THOUGHTS...

_____
_____
_____
_____
_____
_____
_____
_____
_____
_____
_____
_____
_____
_____

DEVELOPING MULTIPLE SOLUTIONS
To Single Problems

WHAT'S THE POINT?

⑥ To help students learn that most problems have more than one solution.

DESCRIPTION OF THE TECHNIQUE:

- Prepare a group of cards. On each card write a typical problem appropriate to students in your age group.
- Divide or allow students to divide themselves into small groups or pairs.
- Have each group take a card. Ask the group to discuss the problem on the card and prepare to discuss or role play the problem and one solution for the class.
- At the end of each scenario involve the class in a discussion of the feasibility of the solution suggested.

⑥ **Variation**

After dividing the class into groups, present all groups with the same problem. Have each group come up with a solution and prepare to discuss or role play it for the class.

⑥ **Variation**

Have one member of the group describe the problem, and then role play only the solution.

PLEASE NOTE!

⑥ **The first group or two you call on set the standard for the behavior of the groups that follow.** So pick your first two groups carefully.

THOUGHTS...

_____
_____
_____
_____
_____
_____
_____
_____
_____
_____
_____
_____
_____
_____

 INCLUSION CONTROL  AFFECTION  COMPETENCY

RESTROOM USE

WHAT'S THE POINT?

⑤ **To provide students with a sense of control and privacy when they need to use the restroom.** Students have the right to use the restroom during the school day as needed. They tend to abuse this privilege only when it is made a major issue.

DESCRIPTION OF THE TECHNIQUE:

⑤ **Young students:**
  • Allow to go as needed.
  • Set up a signal for asking so they are not embarrassed in front of the class.
  • When safety is a concern send with a partner, in small groups, or with an adult.
  • Provide a pass so other adults will know where the kid is headed.

⑤ **Older students:**
  Set up a system that allows students to go as needed. Some ideas are:
  • Hang a clip board or set a stack of passes near the classroom door.
  • Ask students to sign out with their name and the time (get a small stick-on digital clock and glue it above the clip board).
  • Have students jot down their time of return.

PLEASE NOTE!

⑤ **Taking the whole class, a popular elementary technique, assumes that everyone has to go to the bathroom at the same time, deprives kids of an opportunity to develop responsible behavior, and wastes a lot of class time.** Picture the whole staff being told by the principal to go the bathroom at 1:15. Not a pretty thought.

⑤ **In addition to responsible behavior safety and vandalism are always a concern in today's society.** It is important to develop a recording system so that you know who is gone, when they left, when they are expected to return or returned, and how many times a day they were out.

⑤ **Some thoughts we struggle with:**
  • You can't control the kids' bladder and bowels, so don't even try.
  • We're trying to help the kids develop responsible behavior. Letting them determine when they need to go does this.
  • Deal with misbehavior when it happens. Don't assume it's going to.
  • If students choose to go when something important is happening in the classroom, just hold them responsible for taking care of what they missed when they return.
  • Never ever take the doors off the stalls in the bathrooms. Can you imagine using a bathroom without doors?

continued on next page

INCLUSION   CONTROL   AFFECTION   COMPETENCY

THOUGHTS…

CLASSROOM TIME OUT

WHAT'S THE POINT?P

⊚ **To help students learn self control by removing themselves from the group when they are out of control.** This works best when we provide them with a quiet space where they have the opportunity to regroup and get themselves together.

DESCRIPTION OF THE TECHNIQUE:

* Set up a secluded space in the classroom, preferably with a desk and chair.
* Teach students the purpose of the time out spot as in "The time out chair is a place where you can go to get yourself in control when you are out of control."
* Make time out a choice as in "Do you think you can tone it down or do you think you need to go to the time out space for a while?" If the student doesn't tone it down, simply say, "I need you to go to time out."
* The first few times allow the student to determine when he/she feels ready to rejoin the group. After that use a timer and give choices, as in "Five minutes or ten" etc.
* If the student is a frequent 'time outer', develop a signal and eliminate the choice question.
* Refrain from lecturing or moralizing.

PLEASE NOTE!

⊚ **Classroom time outs work best with elementary students.** As described here, it is a time away for the student to engage in thinking. It is not designed to write a plan or do work. If the student is being sent for longer than fifteen minutes it is time for you to move on to another technique. Classroom time outs generally lose their effectiveness after elementary school. See **LEVELS OF TIME OUT** for older students.

THOUGHTS...

_____
_____
_____
_____
_____
_____
_____
_____
_____
_____
_____
_____
_____
_____

 INCLUSION  CONTROL  AFFECTION  COMPETENCY

LEVELS OF TIME-OUT
Squeezing in the Options

 WHAT'S THE POINT?

⑤ **To use levels of "time out" as a way of helping students learn self discipline.** When "time out spots" in the classroom are not producing the desired behavior or if students have reached middle school and peer pressure in the classroom negates this technique, then it is time to think in terms of levels of time out.

 DESCRIPTION OF THE TECHNIQUE:

⑤ **In Place Time Out**
When seen misbehaving, the student is quietly given a choice as in "Do you think you can tone it down or do you need to give this some serious thought?" If the student does not self correct, ask the student to spend a few minutes deciding what he/she is going to do to self correct and to let you know when they have an idea. The student does not have to change location, but should not be involved in classroom activities until an idea has been developed and discussed.

⑤ **Change the Seat Time Out**
As behavior escalates during the period or even over several days, switch to the question, "Do you think you can get it together or would it work better if you changed seats for this period (day)?" If the behavior improves, reinforce quietly with a smile or a few words. If the behavior does not change, ask the student to change seats and prepare to give you an idea on how this behavior will cease to be a problem. Once again, while the student remains in the room, you don't want to involve them in activities until the ideas for change have been discussed.

⑤ **Problem Solving Room Time Out**
As behavior continues to escalate during the period or over several days, quietly tell the student that his/her plan for self correcting is not working and that you need him/her to leave the room. It is best if the student can go to a quiet place, be given time to cool down, then guided by an adult through a problem solving process (several are described in this book). When the student has a self correction plan ready, he/she asks the sending teacher for a re-entry conference. Only after the conference has been held is the student allowed to return to that class.

⑤ **Removal From Building Time Out**
The student has now escalated to the point where the class cannot function and all previous time out levels have produced no behavior change. It is time for the student to go home. This means asking for support from your administrator. The student can be sent home; return next day. If the parents aren't home the author has had great success

continued on next page

delivering them to the one of the parent's place of work (after a phone call of course). The student can also be formally suspended. In any event, it is vital that the student develop a plan for self correction and have a re-entry conference with the sending teacher before coming back to the classroom.

 PLEASE NOTE!

⊚ **Removal from one class, unless it is removal to home, need not keep the student out of his/her other classes.** Being sent to in-school suspension or the problem solving room for the whole day or for several days for getting in trouble with one teacher is reverting to punishment and not conducive to the student owning and solving the original problem.

⊚ **Making a plan for self correction is best done with adult guidance.** Most of us as adults do not sit down and fill out a form when we have a problem. We find a friend or two and talk it over. The same applies to kids. If a form is used at all, it works best to use it after the discussion to formalize the agreement.

⊚ **You say you don't have a Problem Solving Room.** No problem, many schools have had great success turning their in-school suspension or detention rooms into problem solving rooms. Fewer students can be served at a time, but the number of students needing this service tends to decrease.

⊚ **Notice we keep talking about a re-entry conference with the sending teacher.** This is most important and is based on the idea that a problem can only be solved by the people who own the problem. Talking to the principal or the counselor or the **Problem Solving Room** adult can be helpful and even necessary at times. However, to see improvement the crucial talk is the re-entry conference with the sending teacher.

⊚ **While these time out levels have been presented in a sequence, from least intrusive to most intrusive, we discourage thinking of then as a step one, step two, etc. process.** There are no hard and fast rules for how many times **In Place Time Out** can or should be used before going to **Change the Seat Time Out**. Nor is there any hard and fast rule about starting with **In Place Time Out**. With some students you might begin with **Change of Seat Time Out**. The concept here is - you are the professional, students and circumstances differ, use your best judgment.

THOUGHTS…

_____
_____
_____
_____
_____
_____
_____
_____

 INCLUSION CONTROL  AFFECTION  COMPETENCY

✔ ✔✔ ✔

STARTING THE CLASS
A Soft or Hard Beginning?

WHAT'S THE POINT?

⑥ **To get the class off to a solid start everyday.** The first few minutes of the day or of each period set the stage for what is to come. Whether you are task oriented and need or prefer an academic start, or are more into the relationship aspect and need or prefer a social beginning, being aware of what you are trying to accomplish and then carefully planning will just about guarantee a higher rate of success.

DESCRIPTION OF THE TECHNIQUE:

⑥ **Soft Start** (a relationship beginning)
• This start is usually seen in in classes with younger students as in Head Start, prekindergarten, kindergarten and first grade. It can also be effective at any grade level where it is important to focus first on relationship or where the teacher is a relationship type person.
• Allocate a specific amount of time (10 to 15 minutes).
• Roam the room engaging in eye contact, touch, smile, and some conversation with each student.
• Encourage students to interact with each other.
• Teach students to handle tasks such as preparing supplies, hanging up their coats, and going to the lavatory during this time.
• Have centers that students can either be assigned to or choose.

⑥ **Hard Start** (an academic beginning)
• This start is usually seen in grades two, three and up, and where students change classes periodically. It is a task-oriented beginning used by teachers who feel the need for more structure or just want to get right into the meat of the day. However it does not ignore the need for affection.
• Stand in the doorway so that students enter one at a time.
• Make eye contact, touch (if comfortable with), and smile as each student enters.
• The minute the bell rings step into the classroom and start teaching. Engage all students in a group activity that has something to do with academic learning:
  - journal writing
  - a quick quiz
  - a brain teaser
• Take care of housekeeping (lunch count, attendance, etc.), while the students are engaged in the activity.
• Wrap up the activity with students and move right into the lesson.

continued on next page

INCLUSION CONTROL AFFECTION  COMPETENCY

✓ ✓✓ ✓

 PLEASE NOTE!

⊚ **Some definite "do not's":**

- Do not feel you must take roll the first five minutes. Trust me, the secretaries will not die.
- Do not feel you must do the lunch count right away. The cooks may faint, but will survive.
- Do not have your class listen to a voice coming out of the ceiling. Either cut the wire or stuff a sock in it. They can't build a relationship with an intercom.
- Do not turn on the TV. By the time the students leave high school they will have watched some 15,000 hours at home. Give them a break. Try talking with them.

THOUGHTS...

_____
_____
_____
_____
_____
_____
_____
_____
_____
_____
_____
_____
_____
_____
_____
_____
_____
_____
_____
_____
_____
_____
_____
_____
_____
_____
_____
_____
_____
_____
_____
_____
_____

✓✓

LISTEN UP, I'M STARTING THE LESSON
Ways to Get Students' Attention When Beginning a Lesson

WHAT'S THE POINT?

⑥ **To let students know that the lesson is beginning.** Sounds easy but this is one of the most elusive techniques that teachers have to deal with. The main reason that it is so elusive is because how one starts the lesson is highly individualistic and depends heavily on the teacher's personality.

DESCRIPTION OF THE TECHNIQUE:

⑥ **Some teachers do not begin a lesson until all eyes are on them and the room is quiet.** They either stand and wait or walk quietly around the room until they feel they have everyone's attention. If started the first day of school and done consistently, this can be very effective. If not done consistently, this can be disastrous.

⑥ **Some teachers use the spot method.** The teacher always goes to the same spot in the room to begin a lesson. The spot is used for no other kinds of communications.

⑥ **Some teachers use a signal.** Flip the lights, ring a bell, tap the desk, clap a rhythm, yell and scream (No, just kidding). Once again consistency is the key.

⑥ **Some teachers just step into the class and begin teaching.** They use their eyes and the movement of their body around the room while teaching to draw the kids into them. This is effective if you have a patience and persistent personality.

PLEASE NOTE!

⑥ **Consistency is the key.**

THOUGHTS…

_____
_____
_____
_____
_____
_____
_____
_____
_____
_____
_____

✔✔   ✔

PHYSICAL AGGRESSION IN THE CLASSROOM
Younger Children

 WHAT'S THE POINT?

⟳ **To make it clear to students that physical aggression will not be tolerated in the classroom.** Many young children come to us using physical instead of verbal skills to communicate their needs and wants.

 DESCRIPTION OF THE TECHNIQUE:

⟳ **When a young child hits another, promptly and firmly remove the hitter from the area while stating "I can not allow you to hit others".** Put the student in a quiet area away from others to cool off (see **CLASSROOM TIME OUT & LEVELS OF TIME OUT**).

⟳ **When the student is in the thinking state discuss:**
- What happened that led to the incident.
- How he or she feels now.
- How he or she thinks the other person might be feeling.
- What are other choices he or she might have made to solve the problem.
- What he or she plans to do to make amends. (see **THE PROBLEM SOLVING MODEL**).

⟳ **Use books, videos, pictures, and songs to teach about feelings and how to deal appropriately with feelings.** (see **TEACHING KIDS "FEELING" WORDS**).

⟳ Brainstorm and role play ways to handle physical aggression.

 PLEASE NOTE!

⟳ **Reinforce each incident or problem that is solved without physical aggression.** Don't overdo, just say to the student "Doesn't it feel good to handle your problem without using your fists?"

THOUGHTS...

_____
_____
_____
_____
_____
_____
_____
_____
_____
_____

PHYSICAL AGGRESSION IN THE CLASSROOM
Older Students

 WHAT'S THE POINT?

⟲ **To make it clear to students that physical aggression will not be tolerated in the classroom.** Many older kids still come to us using physical instead of verbal skills to communicate their needs and wants.

 DESCRIPTION OF THE TECHNIQUE:

Here are some ideas in use around the country:

⟲ Immediately separate the students involved.

⟲ Send them to a quiet area, a time out room, or the office; a place where they can cool down.

⟲ If it's unprovoked assault or assault with a weapon, many schools either call the police or suspend the student.

⟲ Many schools are now calling the police if there is any blood, regardless of age.

⟲ If it's a severe fight or if the students involved have been involved in numerous fights, many schools suspend.

⟲ Some schools, particularly high schools, have zero tolerance for fighting and suspend whenever one occurs.

⟲ Many schools when the fight is not severe (like pushing, shoving, or name calling) after cool down use student conflict managers or an adult to guide the participants through conflict resolution. (see **THE PROBLEM SOLVING MODEL**).

⟲ Some schools require that all students involved in aggressive behavior take an anger management course.

⟲ <u>The most important point is that no matter how the school decides to handle fights, the students involved need to go through conflict resolution or the problem solving process together before returning to class</u> (see **THE PROBLEM SOLVING MODEL**).

 PLEASE NOTE!

⟲ **When students are punished for fighting instead of being taught a process for handling conflict, the physical aggression will simply continue.** We have to teach to behaviors we want to see in the kids.

 INCLUSION  CONTROL  AFFECTION COMPETENCY

 ✓   ✓✓   ✓

NONVERBAL CLASSROOM MANAGEMENT
Things To Do Before I Open My Mouth

 WHAT'S THE POINT?

⊚ **To develop a variety of nonverbal classroom management techniques; things to do before opening your mouth.**

 DESCRIPTION OF THE TECHNIQUE:

⊚ **Use The Eyes**
- Stand at the door, put a smile on your face, and look in student's eyes as they enter.
- Always position yourself in the room so you can sweep the room with your eyes every 10 to 20 to 30 seconds. The more unruly the class, the more you sweep.
- When students begin to loose control, give them the" look," the "evil eye," before saying anything (see **THE LOOK**). Some students will ignore it, others will self correct (this means straighten up).
- When talking with students one-on-one, especially when the conversation takes place in the classroom and has to do with straightening up, walk up to the student and look into their eyes before you speak.

⊚ **Use The Body**
- Be at the classroom door as students enter and leave. Position yourself so only one student at a time can enter and leave. This gives a brief moment of closeness and intimacy.
- Walk around the classroom as you teach. Stand by all students (not just the ones who make you mad or make you glad) at least once a day or period as you teach.
- Walk toward a student like you like them when you are about to deliver what the student will probably see as a negative message. If you can't walk toward, at least lean in.
- Use proximity. Slowing mosey toward the offending student, not making eye contact, perhaps even backing in. Then stand (or sit) close to the student without saying a word and wait a minute or two to see if the student will self correct.
- Use "slanted body, slanted eyes and bending ever so slightly at the waist". You stand by the student with your body at a slant (or diagonal to the student), not "fronting the student off" as the kids describe it. Then you bend slightly into the student as you talk, your eyes at a slant. This is a more intimate position, not the best, but the best you can do with 20 some other students in the classroom. And by bending slightly at the waist, you can keep your eyes high enough to keep sweeping the room.

⊚ **Use Signals**
- Use your hands to signal gum out, hat off, take a seat, or lips shut.
- Use blinking the lights to signal the need for silence, eyes up here, bodies frozen, etc.

continued on next page

- Write messages on the board. "Thanks for working so well. Papers will be collected in 20 minutes."
- Use cards. Red card hanging means I am talking, no one else talks or leaves the room. Green card hanging means you can work with a partner, talk with others at your table, sharpen your pencil, take the pass and go to the bathroom, etc.

⑥ **Use A Spot**

- Pick a spot on the floor where you always stand when you are giving directions. Try never to give directions until you are on the spot. Pick another spot to use whenever you're giving group "I needs" and "I wills." (see **I NEED AND I WILL**).

PLEASE NOTE!

⑥ **Our most effective techniques in working the classroom are nonverbal.** Most of us don't get in too much trouble until we open our mouths. Thought for the day, keep it shut as long as possible.

THOUGHTS…

_____
_____
_____
_____
_____
_____
_____
_____
_____
_____
_____
_____
_____
_____
_____
_____
_____
_____
_____
_____
_____
_____
_____
_____
_____
_____
_____

THE LOOK
(Also Known as The Evil Eye)

 WHAT'S THE POINT?

⑥ To use eye contact to help students take control of themselves and to help us maintain the control needed to teach.

 DESCRIPTION OF THE TECHNIQUE:

⑥ **In the classroom.**
Give the student THE LOOK. Need we say more? THE LOOK sends the message that I trust you enough and believe in you enough to get it together before I have to do anything else. Use THE LOOK as the first response to all non life threatening behaviors.

⑥ **Around the building.**
Try using THE LOOK as the first response wherever you encounter misbehavior; cafeteria, playground, halls, etc. THE LOOK sends a strong "can do" message.

THOUGHTS...

_____
_____
_____
_____
_____
_____
_____
_____
_____
_____
_____
_____
_____
_____
_____
_____
_____
_____
_____
_____
_____

 INCLUSION  CONTROL  AFFECTION COMPETENCY

THE ART OF ASKING QUESTIONS
Known As Ask Don't Tell

 WHAT'S THE POINT?

⊚ **To get the kids to do more thinking than the adult**. When students tell you, instead of you telling them, the odds for behavior change are increased.

 DESCRIPTION OF THE TECHNIQUE:

⊚ **Avoid your favorite questions.** They only make the student mad.
- **Why**
"Why are you late?" Now be honest, do you really want to know?
- **What should**
"How should you have handled that meeting?" Does "should" motivate you?
- **Sarcasm**
"How many times do I have to tell you?" What if students answered?

⊚ **Give these a try.** They just might work.
- **The point blank question.**
Just ask, "What do you plan to do about this?" Please give this one a try. You might be pleasantly surprised at the really reasonable answers you get.
- **The "yes or no" question**.
"Is this the safe way to play, yes or no?" The idea is to put the struggle in the kid's head.
- **What's your best suggestion?**
"What's your best guess as to what might happen if___?" Just wait and see what they say.

⊚ **Apply to academics.**
- "How many pages do you think it will take to tell the tale?"
- "Who might you ask to give you some ideas?"
- "What do you think you might do to demonstrate you have mastered the concept?"
- "Where do you think you might look to find more information?"

 PLEASE NOTE!

⊚ **You get the idea.** Remember, the question must take the student from this moment forward. The answer needs to come up and out of the student. Think, kid, think!

Based on the materials developed by Jim Fay and Foster W. Cline, M.D. of the Cline/Fay Love and Logic Institute, Inc., Golden, CO. Contact them for materials and speaking at 1-800-455-7557.

 INCLUSION CONTROL  AFFECTION  COMPETENCY

✓✓   ✓

GIVING CHOICES

 WHAT'S THE POINT?

☺ To use choices in the classroom to set your limits and give students the opportunity to make decisions.

 DESCRIPTION OF THE TECHNIQUE:

☺ **Give students two choices, choices that are:**
  - **Acceptable to you.** Don't say, "You can either do your work now or stay in at recess." if you don't want to stay in your self. The student will know they have you.
  - **Enforceable by you.** If you cannot enforce one of the choices, don't give it. Somehow the student always knows and will pick that one just to set you up.

☺ **Never, never say:**
  - **"You have two choices."** Now you are into "you" messages (see **I NEED AND I WILL**) and right back in the power struggle. Just ease into it using statements like "Which would work best for you, ___ or ___?" or "Would you rather ___ or ___?"
  - **You have chosen.** You have given the student two choices as in "Do you think you can tone it down or would it work better if you worked at the back table?" The student says she can tone it down, then continues to act out. When you circle back, do not say "You have now chosen to go to the back table." because this puts you immediately back in a power struggle. Just say, "And what do I need you to do? Go to the back table. Thanks for moving." Saying thanks before they move ups the odds for them moving. Then break eye contact and walk away, the assumption of compliance.

☺ **Make a list of potential choices.**
  - **Use the following worksheet (CHOICES) to make lists of what you can control.** This can be done alone or with your grade level or team members. This sheet does not cover all choice options, but is a good place to start.

☺ **Teach students the art of making choices.** Use the following worksheet (**I HAVE CHOICES**) to help younger students develop the concept of thinking in term of options and choices. With older students come up with some typical situations and individually, in small groups, or with the whole group, brainstorm a list of options or choices they could use in each situation. Be sure to follow through with a discussion of how each choice might work out for them.

THOUGHTS...

_____

_____

_____

_____

_____

_____

Based on the materials developed by Jim Fay and Foster W. Cline, M.D. of the Cline/Fay Love and Logic Institute, Inc., Golden, CO. Contact them for materials or speaking at 1-800-455-7557.

CHOICES
What can I control?

Make a list of all the people you can involve in choices, all the places you can use in choices, and time you can use. Examples: "Do you think you can settle down or do you need to talk with me (people) at recess?" "Do you think you can tone it down or would it work better if you sat at the back of the room (place)?" "Will five or ten minutes in time out (time) help you remember not to shout out?"

PEOPLE	PLACE	TIME

I HAVE CHOICES

Write what is happening in the center of the flower.
Then write the choices you have on the petals.

 INCLUSION CONTROL  AFFECTION COMPETENCY

✔✔

THE CIRCLE ' ROUND TECHNIQUE
A Quick One-On-One Problem Solving Conversation

WHAT'S THE POINT?

⑥ **To engage students in a brief problem solving conference.** As teachers, we have too many problems and too little time. Often we resort to sending a student out of the room or ignoring some behavior that really offends us in the interest of keeping the class going. The problem with these techniques is that the problem is never addressed by the two people who own the problem - the student and us. The following is a technique that has proved helpful when the problem isn't too severe or too frequent.

DESCRIPTION OF THE TECHNIQUE:

⑥ **When we send a student out to be fixed, as to detention or on a referral, when the student returns to us the student returns with the problem firmly in hand.** This is because the only two people who can solve a problem are the two people who own the problem.

⑥ **When a student acts out in class and we ignore the behavior or get it handled but are still upset, when the student comes to us the next day, we still have the problem firmly in hand because our feelings have not been expressed.**

⑥ Therefore, before a student returns after one of the situations above, "Circle "Round."

⑥ **Find a time when you and the student can talk somewhat privately.** Some suggestions are:
  • As the student comes in the door.
  • Asking the student to step in the hall. Start the class and step out in the hall keeping one eye on the class.
  • Using your planning period or lunch period.
  • Before or after school.

⑥ **Ask the student if they have a minute, you would like to talk with them briefly.**

⑥ **Start with a brief "I feel" message.** One simple sentence, no more. "I just wanted to let you know that I did not like the way you yelled at me in class the other day."

⑥ **Follow quickly with a question to get the student involved in thinking.** "Do you think this will be a problem in the future?"

continued on next page

✓✓

🌀 **You will get one of three answers.** Respond as follows.

- Answer one: "No, it won't happen again." Say, "I hope not."
- Answer two: Silence. Wait a moment and then say, "I hope not."
- Answer three: "Who knows. What's it to you anyway." Say, "I hope not."

🌀 **This is a time for hoping.** It's really all you have going for you.

🌀 **Some teachers end with, "Thanks for talking with me."** (even if the student has not said a word).

🌀 **Some even add, "Look forward to seeing you in class."**

 PLEASE NOTE!

🌀 **The point is to have a very brief conversation to clear the air without going into great detail.** With a little practice, **THE CIRCLE 'ROUND TECHNIQUE** can be done in 10 to 20 seconds. Message sent. Message received. Let's get on with class. For more in-depth conversations, see **THE PROBLEM SOLVING MODEL.**

THOUGHTS...

_____
_____
_____
_____
_____
_____
_____
_____
_____
_____
_____
_____
_____
_____
_____
_____
_____
_____
_____
_____
_____
_____
_____
_____

SETTING LIMITS
Getting Kids To Do What They Might Not Want To Do

 WHAT'S THE POINT?

⑥ To get kids to do what you want them to do and what they might not want to do in a manner that supports their proactive (I can be a responsible kid) behavior rather than their reactive (I am just an object being manipulated by my teacher) behavior.

 DESCRIPTION OF THE TECHNIQUE:

⑥ **Be clear about what you want them to do.**
   • I want them to paint pictures without mixing the paints and slopping up the room.
   • I want students to be on time to class.
   • I want students to bring in their homework.

⑥ **Acknowledge to them what you know might happen or what they might really be thinking or wanting to do.**
   • "I know it is sometimes difficult to keep from mixing the paints or spilling some on the floor. Sometimes it is even fun to just slop it around."
   • "I understand that sometimes things happen or you loose track of time and it gets to be hard to be on time."
   • "It is sometimes hard to do your homework when you have soccer, work, etc."

⑥ **Then give them a BRIEF reason for why they might want to do what you want them to do.**
   • "The room needs to be kept clean and the materials organized for the next group of kids who come in."
   • "I give the directions (take the attendance, do the lunch count, give a quiz, etc.) at the beginning of the period and don't want you to miss out."
   • "Students who do their homework on a regular basis learn more and are better prepared to go to the next grade."

 PLEASE NOTE!

⑥ **When used, the results from this way of talking are dramatic.** Kids who feel that the adult at least sort of understands them are more apt to respond with appropriate behavior. It is when they feel they are being controlled that the negative reactions come out. In other words, this is just one more way to avoid the power struggles.

THOUGHTS…

_____

_____

_____

✓✓

REINFORCING THE POSITIVE HALF
Of The Half A _ _ Thing The Student Does

 WHAT'S THE POINT?

6 **To reinforce the positive half of the students behavior.** Kids tend to do things half way or half a _ _. Then we adults have a choice to make. Do we want to reinforce the positive half or the negative half?

 DESCRIPTION OF THE TECHNIQUE:

6 **When the student does something half a _ _ or half way, if you want to set up long term positive change, reinforce the positive half and let go of the negative.** Yes, I said LET IT GO!

6 **Example:** The student cuts in line. You give her the signal to get back in place. The student complies. Do you go into teacher lecture 554 about responsibility and what will happen and how many times you have discussed this, or do you just say "Thanks" and LET IT GO?

6 **Example:** The student owes 6 back homework assignments and turns in 3. Do you go into where is the rest and if it isn't in, etc., or do you just say "Thanks" and LET IT GO?

6 **Example:** You ask a student several times to pick up the mess under his desk. After comments like "This is janitors work" and "I don't have to." the student yells at you in an ugly tone of voice, "Oh, all right. I'll pick it up. Make you happy?" Big decision. Do you go into don't you ever talk to me in that tone of voice, etc., or do you just say "Thanks" and LET IT GO?

 PLEASE NOTE!

6 **Yes, we all would like the student to say, "Oh thanks for reminding me. I'd be more than happy to pick it up."** Life just doesn't go that way. There are times to just take what you can get and LET IT GO. If the behavior really gnaws on you, wait a day or so and talk with them privately. (see **THE CIRCLE 'ROUND TECHNIQUE**).

THOUGHTS...

_____

_____

_____

_____

_____

Based on the materials developed by Jim Fay and Foster W. Cline, M.D. of the Cline/Fay Love and Logic Institute, Inc., Golden, CO. Contact them for materials or speaking at 1-800-455-7557.

SIDESTEPPING MINOR POWER STRUGGLES
Handling Smart Remarks and Eyeball Rolls

 WHAT'S THE POINT?

🌀 To handle smart remarks, eyeball rolls and other annoying things that students do without destroying the relationship or loosing your cool.

 DESCRIPTION OF THE TECHNIQUE:

🌀 **When a student is "messing with your head," you know, just trying to distract you, get you off track, or draw you into an argument, try using the following technique:**
- The student says, "This class sucks."
- Say, "Probably so."
- The student says, "We read this last year."
- Say, "Thanks for sharing that with me."
- The student says, "Why do we have to learn this?"
- Say, "Nice try."

🌀 **You are using negative assertion; agreeing with the negative thing the student just said.** When this is done without sarcasm and followed by redirecting with a comment or a question and then breaking eye contact and walking away, it can be quite effective.

🌀 **The "redirect and walk away":**
- The student says, "I'm not doing any work today and you can't make me."
- Say, "Could be and what did I ask you to do?" and walk away.
- The student rolls the eyes and shakes the head after you have given a direction.
- Say, "Nice try and we are starting on page 54." and walk away.

 PLEASE NOTE!

🌀 **Remember, smart remarks and eyeball rolls are nothing personal.** It's just what kids do to rev up or redirect the adult. This is where the excitement comes in for them. Handle it with a little finesse and lots of humor and life will be better for both of you.

THOUGHTS...

_____
_____
_____
_____
_____
_____
_____
_____
_____

CHAPTER 10

WINNING WAYS
for
AFFECTION

 INCLUSION CONTROL AFFECTION COMPETENCY

✓   ✓   ✓   ✓

MODEL, MODEL, MODEL
Do As I Do

WHAT'S THE POINT?

⑥ **To model on a daily basis the behaviors I want to see in the kids in front of me.**
Teachers who model the behaviors they want, such as being courteous, respecting others, and remaining in control of themselves tend to have classes that exhibit the same behaviors.

DESCRIPTION OF THE TECHNIQUE:

⑥ **Simply show your students through your own behavior how to act in the classroom. Some examples are:**
- Talking in a quiet voice.
- Listening to others.
- Being helpful to others.
- Treating students with respect, regardless of behavior.
- Making eye contact.
- Smiling.
- Keeping personal materials neat and tidy.
- Respecting others' property.
- Treating every student like they're your best friend.
- Leading with empathy.
- Using the problem solving model.
- Showing an interest in every student.
- Using "can do" messages instead of "can't do" messages.

PLEASE NOTE!

⑥ **Modeling is the most powerful behavior you can use in the classroom. Students do as we do, not as we say.** So save your breath and start doing.

THOUGHTS...

_____
_____
_____
_____
_____
_____
_____
_____
_____
_____
_____

INCLUSION  CONTROL AFFECTION  COMPETENCY

✓   ✓✓

WELCOMING NEW STUDENTS

WHAT'S THE POINT?

⊚ **To help students new to the school fit into the routine and develop friendships.**

DESCRIPTION OF THE TECHNIQUE:

⊚ **The following are ideas that have been used successfully in many schools.**

⊚ **Interviewing**
New students are interviewed by a current student. The results of the interview are posted on a central bulletin board (see sample sheets on the next pages), written up in the school paper, shown on the school TV station, broadcast over the school radio, or announced over the school PA system. You might want to check for permission with the student or the students parents before doing some of the above, especially if the information is going outside the school.

⊚ **Buddy System**
A student knowledgeable about the functioning of the school is assigned to the student. They take the new student on a tour of the school, introduce them to the teachers and other students, and in general help them understand what's happening and help them get started.

⊚ **Welcoming Bag**
A bag made of paper, plastic, or canvas or a folder, all printed with the school logo, is handed to the student. This contains all the information the student needs to take home. Some schools include pencils with the school name, crayons, paper for the first day, bumper stickers, or anything that they can identify with the school. These can be prepared in advance. They save hunting through stacks of papers for the forms while the parents and new student wait anxiously in the office. They also make it easier for parent or student to get all the vital papers home.

⊚ **Introducing The School Using Video**
New students and their parents are shown a video that introduces them to many aspects of the school. These are usually made by students using students. They can include any variety of ideas. Some possibilities are a tour of the building, special programs like band and music, expectations for behavior in halls, cafeteria, and assemblies, words of welcome from the principal and some of the teachers, and comments from students on how things really are.

continued on next page

⊚ **Welcoming People**
This is by far the most important. All people who come in contact with the new student and the parents act like they are glad to see them. Enrolling the new student becomes top priority in the office. The receiving teacher(s) welcome the student to class **no matter what**. Statements like "I got the last two students." or "My section is full." are saved for private conversations with the principal later in the day.

 PLEASE NOTE!

⊚ **The first few minutes or hours are perhaps the most important in the career of a student in your school**. The impressions gained and the behavior encountered in those early moments can set the tone for the attitude of the student and the parents and many of the later interactions for as long as the family stays with you.

THOUGHTS...

WELCOME

(paste picture)

Name _____

Advisor _____ Grade _____

Came from _____

Favorite music group _____

Favorite things to do _____

Favorite foods _____

Sports _____

What likes best about new school _____

What misses most about old school _____

I'M HERE!!

(paste picture)

Name _____

Teacher _____ Grade _____

Came from _____

Favorite color_____Favorite food _____

Brothers or sisters _____

Pets _____ Likes to _____

What likes best about new school _____

What misses most about old school _____

 INCLUSION  CONTROL AFFECTION  COMPETENCY

LEAD WITH EMPATHY
And Drop The Sympathy

 WHAT'S THE POINT?

⑥ **To lead with empathy when interacting with students who are having problems and may be (actually often are) in negative emotional states.**

 DESCRIPTION OF THE TECHNIQUE:

⑥ When a student is having a problem and is in a negative emotional state, the adult wants to "lead with empathy;" that is to begin the interaction showing sadness or concern (my concern is always for you) and then acknowledging the feeling(s) the student is experiencing.

⑥ **Leading with empathy allows the pain of what the student has just done or experienced to enter the heart.** For example, the student hits another student. Instead of saying, "That was a dumb thing to do." or "Why did you do that?" for which the student has no answer, you lead with empathy by looking sad and concerned and guessing how the student might be feeling. You say, "You must be really angry?" This is something the student can't argue against and he now believes you understand him. Then you go into problem solving (see **THE PROBLEM SOLVING MODEL**).

⑥ **Nonverbal Empathy**
   • It is not always necessary to say something. Just rearranging your face can send the empathy message. A rule of thumb, when moving toward a student who is engaging in a behavior you do not feel is appropriate, do so with a look of sadness and concern on your face.

⑥ **Verbal Empathy**
   • When the situation is more severe, lead with an empathic statement delivered in a questioning manner. Since you don't know how the student is feeling, you will need to guess.
      - "You must be really upset?"
      - "Feeling really sad and lonely?"
      - "Anxious, huh?"
   • You will get one of four responses:
      - One: You have guessed the feeling. The student's body falls into alignment and the two of you can now talk.
      - Two: The student self corrects. You say, "Feeling sad, huh?" and the student says "No, I'm just upset."
      - Three: The student says nothing. In this case you model what a well put together

continued on next page

emotionally healthy person might be feeling. "If that had happened to me I would be feeling . . ."

    - Four: The student turns on you. "You don't know how I feel. What are you trying to do, use psychology on me?" You respond once again by modeling, "If that had happened to me I probably would be feeling . . ."

• In all cases you then go into problem solving (see **THE PROBLEM SOLVING MODEL**).

 PLEASE NOTE!

⑥ **Leading with empathy, nonverbal or verbal, allows the pain of what the student has just done or experienced to enter the heart and opens the possibility of behavior change.** Try it. You might like it. We know most kids will.

THOUGHTS...

_____
_____
_____
_____
_____
_____
_____
_____
_____
_____
_____
_____
_____
_____
_____
_____
_____
_____
_____
_____
_____
_____
_____
_____
_____
_____
_____
_____
_____
_____
_____
_____
_____
_____
_____

Based on the Problem Solving Model developed by Jim Fay and Foster W. Cline, M.D. of the Cline/Fay Love and Logic Institute, Inc., Golden, CO. Contact them for materials or speaking at 1-800-455-7557.

 **INCLUSION** **CONTROL**  **AFFECTION**  **COMPETENCY**

THE "I NOTICED" ROUTINE

 WHAT'S THE POINT?

⑥ To build the relationship with students by noticing something about them on a regular basis; something they cannot discredit or argue about.

 DESCRIPTION OF THE TECHNIQUE:

⑥ **Pick a student with whom you do not have the best relationship.**

⑥ **Two or three times a week over a period of several weeks, as you see him in the hall or as she enters or leaves the classroom, acknowledge something you have noticed about him.**
  - "I saw you on the playground yesterday."
  - "I noticed you working out with the varsity football team."
  - "I see you are wearing red today."

⑥ **K.I.S.S.: Keep It Simple Sweetheart.** One simple sentence will do.

⑥ **Notice these are factual statements.** There are no value judgments expressed as in "That's a great shirt." Many students who aren't doing well in school can't handle value judgments. They would probably say, "This is just an ugly old shirt. What is my teacher trying to do?"

⑥ **Ideas for gathering "I noticed" statements:**
  - Take 5 minutes a week and swing through the cafeteria while the students are eating.
  - Take 5 minutes once a week and walk around the playground. The exercise will do you good if nothing else.
  - Stand at your door each passing time with one eye on the hall.
  - Go to school games or concerts. You don't have to stay the whole time, just long enough to see and be seen.

⑥ **Variation**
  When a student is having trouble with several teachers, have each teacher do this on a regular basis. The student's work may not improve but the relationship will get better and that is a first step in the right direction.

 PLEASE NOTE!

⑥ **We all like to be noticed.** When I (Betsy) was looking to hire a new teachers, I liked to interview substitutes who had been successful in our building. The substitute teachers who finished their day in our building by finding me before they went home, introducing themselves one more time, and then saying something positive about their experience with our kids, were always the first faces that came to mind. You can call it brown nosing or sucking up, but the technique has merit in terms of relationship building.

Based on the materials developed by Jim Fay and Foster W. Cline, M.D. of the Cline/Fay Love and Logic Institute, Inc., Golden, CO. Contact them for materials or speaking at 1-800-455-7557.

✓✓

GETTING TO KNOW
What Students Think of Me

WHAT'S THE POINT?

⑥ **To get periodic input from students on my behavior.** In the words of Robert Bush, author of The Teacher-Pupil Relationship:

"Teachers retain their effectiveness as professional persons only so long as they remain warmly human, sensitive to the personal needs of children, and skillful in establishing effective relationships with them."

⑥ Getting regular feedback is one way to know if you are on track.

DESCRIPTION OF THE TECHNIQUE:

⑥ Design or reprint from the following pages some short simple surveys to collect student ideas about your classroom behavior.
⑥ Administer to students on a regular basis.
⑥ When you're feeling strong review the sheets.
⑥ This is the tough part. Adjust your behavior accordingly.

THOUGHTS...

_____
_____
_____
_____
_____
_____
_____
_____
_____
_____
_____
_____
_____
_____
_____
_____
_____
_____
_____

MY TEACHER IS

Circle in **RED** if the words describe your teacher most of the time.

Circle in **BLUE** if the words describe your teacher some of the time.

Circle in **YELLOW** if the words hardly ever describe your teacher.

mean	fun	friendly	boring
loving	respectful	fair	grouchy
strict	understanding	listens	exciting
good sport	great ideas	friendly	humorous
helpful	interesting	cruel	has favorites
organized	problem solver	grouchy	unfair
disorganized	loves teaching	smart	respectful
good friend	flexible	disrespectful	no time for kids

LET ME KNOW
How You Feel About Me As A Teacher

1.	Do I treat students fairly?	Yes	No
2.	Do I help you solve problems?	Yes	No
3.	Am I patient?	Yes	No
4.	Do I yell?	Yes	No
5.	Do I treat you with respect?	Yes	No
6.	Do I follow through on things I tell you?	Yes	No
7.	Do I listen to students?	Yes	No
8.	Do I have a good sense of humor?	Yes	No
9.	Am I friendly?	Yes	No
10.	Do I embarrass you?	Yes	No
11.	Do I smile at you?	Yes	No
12.	Can you trust me?	Yes	No

⊚ **Talk to me.**

List some concerns, ideas, or questions that you have about me as your teacher.

_____
_____
_____
_____
_____
_____
_____
_____
_____
_____
_____
_____
_____
_____
_____
_____
_____

HELP ME UNDERSTAND
How You Feel About Me As A Teacher

1. Do I help you when you need it?   Yes   No

2. Do I give you helpful feedback?   Yes   No

3. Do I think you can do your work?   Yes   No

4. Do I look at you when I talk to you?   Yes   No

5. Do I listen when you want to talk?   Yes   No

6. Do I admit when I don't know?   Yes   No

7. Do I admit when I am wrong?   Yes   No

8. Do you think I'm too strict?   Yes   No

9. Do I share my feelings?   Yes   No

10. Do I recognize you for good work?   Yes   No

11. Are you excited about learning?   Yes   No

12. Am I understanding?   Yes   No

My teacher is:

_____

_____

_____

_____

_____

_____

_____

_____

_____

_____

_____

_____

_____

_____

_____

_____

_____

_____

  ✔ ✔✔

HELPING STUDENTS UNDERSTAND "FUZZY" WORDS AND CONCEPTS

Respect, Responsible, Good Citizen, Good Learner, Cooperation, etc.

 WHAT'S THE POINT?

⑥ **To help students understand the meaning of words and concepts that are hard to define in a sentence or two.** The authors call them "fuzzy" words because they have different meanings for different people. For example, what "respectful" behavior is to one teacher many be quite different to another.

 DESCRIPTION OF THE TECHNIQUE:

⑥ **Choose the word, phrase or concept to be defined.**
⑥ **Using the board or butcher paper, create three columns.**
⑥ **Label the columns "Looks Like", "Sounds Like", and "Feels Like".**
⑥ **With students, brainstorm specific behaviors and feelings for the three columns.** For example "respect" might look like sharing a spare pencil with a friend; might sound like "May I please borrow a pencil.", and might feel like happiness in the pit of your stomach.

⑥ **Variations**
- Change the sheet heading to say, does not look like, sound like or feel like.
- Have students work on sheets in small groups and then share with the class.
- Use with individual students when there have been problems and the students promises to "be good" or "study harder."
- Use this technique at the beginning of the year to involve students in establishing classroom standards for the year.
- Use this technique during the year when there have been group problems like being disrespectful with the substitute.
- Use this technique individually or with the class to teach social skills.

THOUGHTS...

_____
_____
_____
_____
_____
_____
_____
_____
_____
_____

MY COMMITMENT TO CHANGE

When I am:

_____

(being respectful, studying harder, being good, etc.)

I will:

LOOK LIKE You will see me:	SOUND LIKE You will hear me:	FEEL LIKE I will be feeling:

Signed _____ Dated _____

 INCLUSION  CONTROL  AFFECTION  COMPETENCY

CHECKING OUT HOW KIDS ARE FEELING
Instead of Assuming

WHAT'S THE POINT?

⊚ **To verify verbally with students how they are really feeling.** So often we jump to conclusions. We're so sure we know.

DESCRIPTION OF THE TECHNIQUE:

⊚ **When you notice positive or negative body language in your students, instead of assuming you know how they are feeling, ask.**

⊚ **Positive Body Language**
  • "You're looking pretty perky today. I see a big smile and a bounce in your step."

⊚ **Negative Body Language**
  • "I noticed that you look upset. Your fists are gripped and your head is down."

⊚ **Follow Up With:**
  • "Would you like to talk about it?"
  • "Is everything OK?"
  • "I'm here for you if you need to talk."
  • "Tell me more about how you're feeling."

THOUGHTS...

_____
_____
_____
_____
_____
_____
_____
_____
_____
_____
_____
_____
_____
_____
_____
_____
_____

TEACHING KIDS "FEELING" WORDS

 WHAT'S THE POINT?

🌀 **To help students develop a vocabulary of "feeling" words.** Many students and adults have a very limited vocabulary of "feeling" words thus limiting their ability to adequately express their emotions.

 DESCRIPTION OF THE TECHNIQUE:

🌀 Model, model, model. Be aware of how many "feeling" words you use as you talk with students. Are you in a three or four "feeling" words rut?

🌀 Teach "feeling" vocabulary development as a lesson. This is not something that can be left to chance.

🌀 Some ideas seen in schools around the country are:

- For very young children, have them draw faces to match the feelings (see the following worksheet **DRAWING FEELINGS**). You write the "feeling" words or have them copy from the board.

- Give young students a situation and have them draw how they are feeling. You then write the "feeling" words they dictate to you. This is a good one to use when the student has gotten in trouble with you or another student (see **HERE'S WHAT HAPPENED** worksheet).

- For older students, and this can be used with adults too, you give the situation and have the students list as many "feeling" words as possible to go with each situation (see the following worksheets **SITUATIONS AND FEELINGS** and **WHAT AM I REALLY FEELING WHEN**). Retrieval charts that can be left hanging up for a period of time work well here.

 PLEASE NOTE!

🌀 **The ability to express our feelings to ourselves and others is a major step in the positive management of these feelings.** As our friends, John Crumbly, John Aarons, and Wade Fraser, who do wonderful work teaching anger management to angry youth in Eugene, Oregon, say, "The young men come to our program with basically three words for expressing their feelings; sad, mad, and horny." No wonder they are in trouble.

THOUGHTS...

_____
_____
_____
_____
_____
_____
_____
_____
_____

DRAWING FEELINGS

_____

_____

_____

_____

_____

_____

WHAT I AM REALLY FEELING WHEN

When you use each of the expressions below, write as many words as you can to express how you might really be feeling. A few examples have been given for each expression. There are no right and wrong answers, only how you feel.

No One Likes Me	**I Can Do It**	**I Can't**
hurt	*strong*	*lazy*
abandoned	*confident*	*worried*

You Can't Make Me	**I Did It**	**Make Me**
frustrated	*satisfied*	*afraid*
troubled	*relaxed*	*inadequate*

They're Not Like Me	**I'm the Greatest**	**Forget You**
odd	*powerful*	*cheated*
conspicuous	*strong*	*jealous*

SITUATIONS AND FEELINGS

The person next to me keeps trying to copy the test answers off my paper.

_____

She said she was my best friend and now she won't talk to me.

_____

I always get picked last when we pick teams in gym.

_____

No matter how hard I try, I always get bad grades.

_____

My teacher always holds my papers up and tells the class how great they are.

_____

My parents say never smoke, but all my friends are trying to get me to start.

_____

STOPPING PUTDOWNS IN YOUR CLASS
The Tongue Can Be Mightier Than The Sword

WHAT'S THE POINT?

☉ **To help students understand the negative effects of put downs, and that put downs won't be tolerated in your class.**

DESCRIPTION OF THE TECHNIQUE:

☉ **Put Down Prevention**
- Use class meeting time to discuss with students reasons people put each other down.
- Have students keep a record of when and why they put others down, and when they are put down by others. Then discuss.
- Relate putting down to the adult world. Then ask students how this technique will work in a job setting, with a spouse, or with their friends.
- Provide a regular time for students to share their appreciation of others. Some ideas include:
  - Feature Student of the Week when each student writes something nice about the featured student.
  - Class meeting when each student says something nice about someone else.
- Model, model, model. Use positive statements as often as possible.

☉ **Zero Tolerance Policy**
- The first time a student does a put down ask him or her "Is this acceptable in this classroom, yes or no? Can I trust you not to do it again?"
- If it happens a second time with the same student move in with some choices that are acceptable in your school such as, "Do you think you can drop these comments or do you think (one of the following) will help you remember not to?"
  - Time in detention or after school to think it over.
  - Removal from the classroom until the student can convince you he won't do it again.
  - Phone call to the parents to enlist their support in eliminating put downs.
  - A one on one problem solving conference with you (see **THE PROBLEM SOLVING MODEL**).
- If it happens again, follow through.
- Whether it is the first or second time the student will be expected to make amends to the other student before continuing with regular classroom activities. It works best if you ask students how they plan to make amends, rather than telling them that they have to apologize (once again see **THE PROBLEM SOLVING MODEL**).

PLEASE NOTE!

☉ **The point is to develop from the first moment of the first day a zero tolerance for put downs.** It's a problem that only gets worse with time. As students become older, the put-down problem becomes more intense. Put downs are associated with gang involvement, poor self esteem, gaining power, and seeking revenge. The problem can become so acute that it can drive some students from the school.

 INCLUSION  CONTROL  AFFECTION COMPETENCY

 ✓   ✓✓

HANDLING NOTE WRITING
It Is A Communication Skill

 WHAT'S THE POINT?

🌀 **To deal with the disruption of note writing in a positive and non-judgmental way.** We constantly encourage children to hone their writing and communication skills. Isn't it ironic that their note writing sends us into orbit.

 DESCRIPTION OF THE TECHNIQUE:

🌀 Think through before the school year starts how you plan to handle note writing (see **STARTING THE SCHOOL YEAR RIGHT**) for ideas on how to plan and teach.

🌀 Some ideas that have been used successfully by teachers include:
- Ignore it, after all they are writing.
- Be straight forward. Simply say, "I'd appreciate it if you would put it away."
- Walk up to the student and quietly asking them to hand it to you and then throw it away without reading or commenting
- State what you will be doing such as "I'll be collecting all finished papers at the end of the period. Hope yours is one." This leaves it up to them to decide whether they want to write notes or write their report.
- Use humor. Write a note to the note writer asking him or her to stop. Have a student seated near the note writer deliver it. This works especially well with girls.

🌀 After determining how you plan to handle notes, just do it.

 PLEASE NOTE!

🌀 **The idea is to not embarrass the student and/or get into a big power struggle over a note.** We have all been guilty of writing notes during staff meetings. A gentle solution works best for us. Why not try it with one of your students?

💭 **THOUGHTS...**

_____
_____
_____
_____
_____
_____
_____
_____
_____
_____
_____
_____
_____

 INCLUSION  CONTROL AFFECTION  COMPETENCY

✓   ✓✓

TRUE VALENTINE'S DAY ACTIVITIES
Shifting The Focus From Receiving To Giving

 WHAT'S THE POINT?

⑥ To help students understand that Valentine's Day is more than counting the number of Valentines you get in your special envelope.

 DESCRIPTION OF THE TECHNIQUE:

⑥ The following are tried and true activities used by the authors.

⑥ **One Special Valentine**
Cut out one large valentine for every student in the class and one for you. Put or have the students put their name on one heart. Then pass the hearts around the room and have each student write something nice about every other student and sign their name. This can be done as a "when you finish your work" activity or as a whole group class activity. On Valentine's Day, each student goes home with a big heart with messages from the whole class.

⑥ **Variation**
Do the same with the staff at a special Valentine's Day faculty meeting.

⑥ **Partner Class Valentines**
Classes that have a partner class in the same building (a 5th grade class partnered with a 2nd grade class) partner up individually and the partners from each room (a 5th grader and a 2nd grader) make and exchange Valentines.

⑥ **Variation**
The same can be done when classes have a partner class in another school building, in another district, or even a sister city school in another country.

⑥ **Nursing Homes, Retirement Homes, Hospitals**
Classes develop an affiliation with a nursing home, hospital, Meals On Wheels, etc. and make Valentines for the people. When possible, it is best to get names and address each valentine to a specific person.

 PLEASE NOTE!

⑥ **The purpose of these activities is to switch the emphasis from "me to thee."** This is also helpful in areas where children don't have the resources or the home support to get Valentines for every member of the class or where teachers aren't able to ensure that every student gets one from every other student and thus feel left out.

ENDING THE YEAR ON A POSITIVE NOTE
Good-Bye Rituals For That Last Day

 WHAT'S THE POINT?

⑥ To end the school year with a special ritual that sends kids home for the summer with a warm glow in their hearts knowing that their teachers and their peers think of them as special friends.

 DESCRIPTION OF THE TECHNIQUE:

⑥ The following is a collection of tried and true ideas collected over the years from many teachers and schools.

⑥ **Autograph/Memory Book**
Students are given a book for collecting autographs from teachers and students and recording some of their better memories from the year (see the following pages for one you can copy).

⑥ **Memory Page**
Each student is given a large sheet of drawing paper and puts their name on it. Then the sheets are passed around the room so each student can write something or draw something about every other student in the room. This can be done as a "when you finish your work" activity the last week of school or with a timer on the last day (every three minutes we pass the papers on).

⑥ **Class Celebrations**
By class or by grade level, students gather for the last 45 minutes or so of the last day for treats and time to get their autograph or memory books signed.

⑥ **Clap On**
All the students in the school line the halls. The class leaving the building (as in fifth graders going on to middle school) go by in single file and the rest of the student body "claps them on".

continued on next page

 INCLUSION  CONTROL  AFFECTION COMPETENCY

 ✔ ✔✔

⑥ Low Key Graduation for Elementary and Middle Schools
A simple ceremony is held the last 45 minutes or so of the last period of the last day of the school year for the class leaving to go on to the next building. The school song is sung, the cheer led, the creed recited. The principal or one of the teachers calls the students one at a time across the stage and presents them with a certificate stating they have completed the years in this building and are ready to go on. Then students are turned loose to get punch and cookies or ice cream sundaes while they mill about and get their autograph or memory books signed. When the final bell rings, they go home as usual. Many schools invite the parents. No special awards are given at this time. The point is to send every student forth feeling special, not just a special few.

THOUGHTS...

_____
_____
_____
_____
_____
_____
_____
_____
_____
_____
_____
_____
_____
_____
_____
_____
_____
_____
_____
_____
_____
_____
_____
_____
_____
_____
_____
_____
_____
_____
_____
_____
_____
_____
_____
_____
_____

Color It a Great Year!

A Memory Book

Submitted by Judy Baker, Washington Grade School, Vernonia, OR

Cartoon of Funniest Thing
That Happened This Year

Name _____

Grade _____

School Year _____

Teacher _____

Teachers' Autographs

Unforgettable Events

1. _____

2. _____

3. _____

4. _____

5. _____

One thing I'd never change about this year is . . . .

_____

_____

_____

_____

_____

Forgettable Events

1. _____

2. _____

3. _____

4. _____

5. _____

One thing I' wish I could change about this year is . . . .

_____

_____

_____

_____

_____

My Favorite Subject

Read All About It

A Real Toughie!

I Hope Next Year I . . . _____

Did I Ever Grow Up This Year!

Read All About It

I Hope That Next Year I . . .

My Favorite Subject

CHAPTER 11

WINNING WAYS

for

COMPETENCY

 INCLUSION CONTROL  AFFECTION COMPETENCY

MODEL, MODEL, MODEL
Do As I Do

 WHAT'S THE POINT?

⊚ **To model on a daily basis the behaviors I want to see in the kids in front of me.** Teachers who model the behaviors they want, such as being courteous, respecting others, and remaining in control of themselves tend to have classes that exhibit the same behaviors.

 DESCRIPTION OF THE TECHNIQUE:

⊚ **Simply show your students through your own behavior how to act in the classroom. Some examples are:**
- Talking in a quiet voice.
- Listening to others.
- Being helpful to others.
- Treating students with respect, regardless of behavior.
- Making eye contact.
- Smiling.
- Keeping personal materials neat and tidy.
- Respecting others' property.
- Treating every student like they're your best friend.
- Leading with empathy.
- Using the problem solving model.
- Showing an interest in every student.
- Using "can do" messages instead of "can't do" messages.

 PLEASE NOTE!

⊚ **Modeling is the most powerful behavior you can use in the classroom. Students do as we do, not as we say.** So save your breath and start doing.

THOUGHTS...

_____
_____
_____
_____
_____
_____
_____
_____
_____
_____
_____
_____

 INCLUSION  CONTROL  AFFECTION COMPETENCY

✓ ✓✓

ACTIVELY ENGAGING STUDENTS
An Overview for Getting Kids Involved

 WHAT'S THE POINT?

⑥ **To design classroom activities that up the odds for getting kids actively involved.**
We don't need to tell you that students who are not participating in your activities are participating in activities of their own design.

 DESCRIPTION OF THE TECHNIQUE:

⑥ **Thoughts for engaging students in active learning.**
- Let the students in on the purpose for each lesson.
- Relate the lesson to something in their life.
- Remember that students learn in different ways, so vary each lesson's activities to address the different learning styles.
- Give immediate as well as long term feedback.
- Encourage kids to work together as well as individually.
- Make sure all kids experience some success each day.
- Try integrated or thematic units rather than one subject lessons.
- Provide activities at various ability levels for each concept.
- Do more asking than telling.
- Provide lots of opportunities for decision making and choosing.
- Involve kids in designing the lessons and the evaluations.

 PLEASE NOTE!

- Look through this book for **WINNING WAYS** to give you ideas for each of the above points.

THOUGHTS...

_____
_____
_____
_____
_____
_____
_____
_____
_____
_____
_____
_____
_____

WORKING IN PAIRS

WHAT'S THE POINT?

🌀 **To designate specific tasks or times of the day when students can work in pairs.** Contrary to the way many of us were taught, students working with students can raise the achievement of all involved. Paired working also helps break down barriers between students and develop that community feeling.

DESCRIPTION OF THE TECHNIQUE:

🌀 **Turn to Your Neighbor Pairs**
- As you are teaching, stop every so often and ask students to turn to their partner and:
  - discuss a point
  - summarize what has been said so far
  - answer a question
  - design a question
  - solve a problem

🌀 **Write and Edit Pairs**
- Have each student write a composition. Then ask them to trade papers and edit each others paper. After editing, trade back, discuss, and then correct.
- Partner 1 describes to Partner 2 ideas for a composition. Partner 2 makes an outline. The process is reversed. When both partners have an outline, they each write a composition based on the ideas their partner outlined using that outline. Then they trade again and edit each others composition. After editing, they trade back, discuss, and correct.

🌀 **Note-Taking Pairs**
- When showing a film or giving a lecture where students are expected to take notes, ask both partners to take notes. Then, stopping every ten minutes or so, or at the end of the film or lecture, have them share their notes. Ask them to look for something they can take from the other person's notes that they may have missed. This way both sets of notes are improved.

🌀 **Read and Explain Pairs**
- Have one student read and the other summarize.
- Have both students read. Then one summarizes and the other listens for accuracy.
- Have one student read only the heading and the other the body of the text (this is especially helpful when pairing high and low readers).

🌀 **Math Problem-Solving Pairs**
- Have pairs solve one or more math problems. Ask them to come up with one answer and a defense or rational for that answer.

continued on next page

- Have students do the math assignment individually. Then ask them to compare answers and work together on any problems where the answers don't agree until they can come up with one they can both agree on.

🌀 **Drill-Review Pairs**
- Pairs are asked to drill each other on any number of things:
    - spelling words
    - lines in a play
    - a poem to be memorized
    - times tables

🌀 **Debate Pairs**
- The pairs are given a controversial topic. They are each asked to take a side and prepare a defense for that side. They are asked to present their arguments to each other and see if they can convince their partner of the merits of their point of view.

PLEASE NOTE!

🌀 **There really are no hard and fast rules.** There are times when you might want to assign pairs. For example, you want a strong student to work with one with weaker skills. Two points to keep in mind. First, people assigned to a group generally see other groups as better than theirs and want to switch. Second, variety is truly the spice of life. You pick sometimes; they pick sometimes.

There are as many variations of each of these ideas as you (or the students) have imagination. The concept to keep in mind is that students working together and learning together tends to help everyone involved achieve at a higher level.

THOUGHTS...

_____
_____
_____
_____
_____
_____
_____
_____
_____
_____
_____
_____
_____
_____
_____
_____
_____
_____

INCLUSION CONTROL AFFECTION COMPETENCY

TEACHING TO ALL LEARNING STYLES

WHAT'S THE POINT?

⑥ **To design lessons so that students can experience success no matter what their learning style**. Kids come to us with different ways of learning. They have a style that works best for them. We come to teaching with different teaching styles. We tend to teach from our own style. When we go beyond our own style and design lessons that speak to all four styles, we up the odds for greater success with all students. We also add variety to the lessons and make the day more interesting for everyone.

DESCRIPTION OF THE TECHNIQUE:

⑥ Generally speaking kids come to us with one of four learning styles (see following pages). We will call the styles PROMOTER, SUPPORTER, ANALYZER and CONTROLLER. As you observe your students, see if you can detect their style.
- Teaching and learning styles tend to be one and the same. As you look at the characteristics of each style, can you figure out which style is mainly you?
- Study the four sections for each style; (1) characteristics, (2) situations where students excel, (3) situations where students feel stifled, and (4) learning activities that promote learning.
- Design your plan for the day, the week, the concept, or the unit so that you include activities from each style in your plan (see following **Sample Lesson Plan Format**). This will insure that all students have something to look forward to that works for them. It will also up the odds for all students experiencing greater success.

PLEASE NOTE!

⑥ **Experts say styles are not developed until middle or late elementary.** While most teachers can spot the general direction a student is taking, sometimes as early as kindergarten, testing and labeling too early can be unhealthy. Just keep in mind that identifying each student's style is really not the main issue. Since we know that we have students in our classrooms with all styles, what we want to concentrate on is developing our lessons to teach to each style.

THOUGHTS...

_____
_____
_____
_____
_____
_____
_____
_____
_____

PROMOTER
A High Energy, Imaginative Teaching/Learning Style

⑥ **CHARACTERISTICS**
- ease in making decisions
- warmth, friendliness
- flexibility
- creativity, imagination
- insightfulness
- out front behavior, forcefulness
- communicates well

⑥ **SITUATIONS WHERE STUDENTS EXCEL**
- people are involved like in committee work
- new possibilities can be brainstormed
- there is definite structure with boundaries
- follow-through is enforced by someone else
- inspirations are allowed and encouraged
- there is a lot of attention
- they can talk about what is learned
- there is action-oriented activity, as in role playing, drama
- the environment is optimistic, changing
- there is an atmosphere of warmth and friendliness

⑥ **SITUATIONS WHERE STUDENTS FEEL STIFLED**
- physical activity is restrained
- tasks are analytical, systematize and/or disciplined
- there are many logical, detailed presentations - they just want the bottom line
- there is only routine and no room for adventure and action
- they are allowed to go any which way on a project without understood boundaries

⑥ **LEARNING ACTIVITIES THAT PROMOTE LEARNING**
- to the point and ask for bold and opinionated expressions of viewpoints
- concerned with interesting issues that are exciting and forward looking into the future
- debate, presentations, controversy, rebuttals
- mazes, riddles, puzzles
- parades and productions such as "Classroom 220/20" or "News in Review"
- activities that provide a spotlight and attention
- brainstorming (loves this)
- art displays and developing materials to "promote" learning activities
- plays and mime - creative dramatics
- open-ended activities

SUPPORTER
An Easy-Going, People Oriented Teaching/Learning Style

⑥ **CHARACTERISTICS**
- good listener
- concern for fairness
- friendly, likes people
- dislikes conflict
- values friendships
- allows others to initiate
- puts others at ease
- takes directions well

⑥ **SITUATIONS WHERE STUDENTS EXCEL**
- they can please others
- harmony, respect, and good feelings exist
- learning is on facts and about people and living things
- ideals and values are respected
- structure, supervision, and guidance is available
- there is much reassurance, support and personal attention
- ideas can be developed that benefit others
- relationship skills can be applied to get the job done
- committee work, peer tutoring, team building
- ethics are practiced
- their loyalty is valued

⑥ **SITUATIONS WHERE STUDENTS FEEL STIFLED**
- expediency or competition is the main motivational device
- they are left to their own direction
- task achievement is the dominate goal
- socializing is not allowed
- conflict is normal

⑥ **LEARNING ACTIVITIES THAT PROMOTE LEARNING**
- teacher directed activities
- peer tutoring and cross-age activities
- creating stories, poems, and songs
- artwork illustrating people and animals
- role play and creative dramatics
- keeping/reading diaries and journals
- biographies and autobiographies
- philosophy, ecology, psychology, sociology
- organizing learning center materials so that they address all the needs of all learners in their classrooms

ANALYZER
A Thoughtful, Detail Conscious, Task Oriented Teaching/Learning Style

⑥ **CHARACTERISTICS**
- thrives on facts, concepts
- systematic, orderly
- pays attention to detail
- quietly non-threatening
- allows others to initiate
- problem solver
- goal oriented (slowly, carefully)
- persistent
- serious

⑥ **SITUATIONS WHERE STUDENTS EXCEL**
- they can work by themselves
- it is unemotional, factual, practical
- there is freedom to ponder
- the leader give a systematic, structured framework
- routine is the watch word
- there is a lack of pressure
- much attention is given to task results
- value is placed on accumulation of facts
- they can save face when they may be wrong
- there are rules for dealing with others

⑥ **SITUATIONS WHERE STUDENTS FEEL STIFLED**
- little organization exists (teachers wing it)
- nobody reaches out to them
- inconsistency is routine
- pressure abounds
- loud, multi-stimulating activity exists
- the leader is dominating and controlling
- decisions are not based on facts

⑥ **LEARNING ACTIVITIES THAT PROMOTE LEARNING**
- individual reports
- cartoons
- self-directed learning activities
- research activities
- categorizing concepts, events, materials, etc.
- collections and displays
- penmanship or other finely detailed work
- wood carving, model building, miniature displays
- analyzing data and collecting information

CONTROLLER
A Confident, Well-Organized, Task Oriented Teaching/Learning Style

⑥ **CHARACTERISTICS**
- ease, rapidity in decision making
- strong willpower
- capacity performance
- quick responses
- competitiveness
- thorough persistence
- eager ambition
- makes good use of time
- likes workable, logical solutions

⑥ **SITUATIONS WHERE STUDENTS EXCEL**
- organization abounds and is value
- they are allowed to take responsibility and leadership
- it is fast moving and challenging
- there is a change to assume a leadership role
- competition abounds
- there is freedom to accomplish tasks their own way
- there is established authority to respect
- academic achievement is highly valued

⑥ **SITUATIONS WHERE STUDENTS FEEL STIFLED**
- the situation is not under their control
- their goals are thwarted
- it is not fast moving
- teachers wing it
- there are many distractions
- no one appears to be in charge

⑥ **LEARNING ACTIVITIES THAT PROMOTE LEARNING**
- spelling bees
- timed math drills
- sports and play days
- map-making
- grades and goal achievement
- designing and playing instructional games
- leading classroom discussions and project committees
- debates
- projects and reports that require good organizational skills
- special notebooks that organize concepts and activities

 INCLUSION  CONTROL  AFFECTION COMPETENCY

SELECTING THE BEST TEACHING METHOD
Teaching So Kids Will Learn and Remember

 WHAT'S THE POINT?

☙ To select the teaching methods that up the odds for producing responsible, independent learners who not only learn, but remember and apply what they have learned.

Children learn:
- 10% of what the read.
- 20% of what they hear.
- 30% of what they see.
- 50% of what they see and hear.
- 70% of what they say in their own words.
- 90% of what they say while they are doing something.

 DESCRIPTION OF THE TECHNIQUE:

☙ Study the figure below. Choose your teaching methods accordingly.

HIERARCHY OF TEACHING METHODS

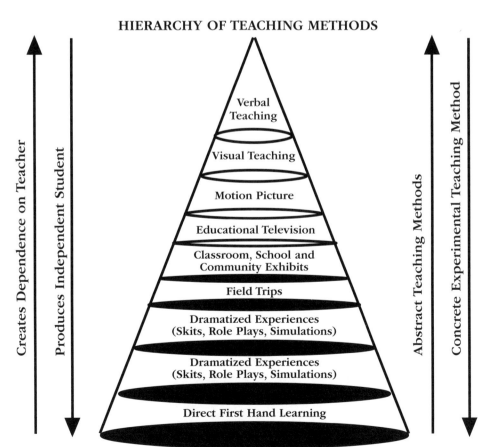

SAMPLE LESSON PLAN FORMAT

Name _____

Grade _____

Subject _____

THE WEEK'S CONCEPT/GOAL/OBJECTIVE
(This can be done by the lesson, the period, the concept, or the unit of study)

⊚ MONDAY
Learning Style _____

Lesson Plan Activities _____

_____

⊚ TUESDAY
Learning Style _____

Lesson Plan Activities _____

_____

⊚ WEDNESDAY
Learning Style _____

Lesson Plan Activities _____

_____

⊚ THURSDAY
Learning Style _____

Lesson Plan Activities _____

_____

⊚ FRIDAY
Learning Style _____

Lesson Plan Activities _____

_____

 INCLUSION  CONTROL  AFFECTION  COMPETENCY

✔   ✔   ✔✔

PARTICIPATORY CLASSROOM TEACHING
Focus on Curriculum

 WHAT'S THE POINT?

⚅ **To give the students significant input into what happens in the classroom while using the curriculum mandated by the district and the state.** So often it seems that we as individual teachers can't make changes because of bureaucracy mandates. Yet we know that students need to see meaning and be involved in the daily decision making if they are to achieve according to ability and stay in school. This is an idea that addresses these needs and can be adapted to any grade level, full day or period by period scheduling, and any community.

 DESCRIPTION OF THE TECHNIQUE:

⚅ **Before or on the first day of class divide the class into homogeneous small groups of three or four students.**
- Develop a list of tasks that can be done by the students. You need enough tasks so each group can be assigned one. Some examples are:
  - design, test, grade, and retest in designated subject areas
  - be responsible for weekly current events discussions
  - room maintenance
  - field trip planning
  - collection and distribution of materials including homework, field trip forms, etc.
  - care of plants and pets
  - snacks as an economic project
  - room store as an economic project
- Assign each group a task and keep them on that task for at least one week.
- Keep the groups intact through a complete rotation of the tasks. Then regroup and do the complete rotation again. Repeat until the end of the year. Drop or add tasks as needed.
- Begin with non-stress, non-academic team building activities when:
  - beginning the year
  - changing groups
  - a new student enters a group
- Hold class meetings or class discussions periodically to discuss problems and concerns.

THOUGHTS...

_____
_____
_____
_____
_____

 INCLUSION  CONTROL  AFFECTION  COMPETENCY

✓ ✓✓

JIGSAW

 WHAT'S THE POINT?

⑥ To create positive interdependence among students while teaching content and developing social skills.

 DESCRIPTION OF THE TECHNIQUE:

⑥ Decide what you are going to teach.
⑥ Prepare the materials to be used.
⑥ Set up the Cooperative Groups (you assign or they form).

⑥ **Variation**

Give each person in the group only part of the information. Group members are responsible for learning their material, teaching it to the other members of the group, and learning what the other members have to teach. A test or culminating activity can be used at the end to determine how much each individual member of the group has learned.

⑥ **Variation**

Divide up the equipment as in a science project so that students are forced to cooperate in order to complete the experiment.

⑥ **Variation**

Group members can be asked to contribute to a single project. For example, a sentence to a paragraph, an article to a newsletter, a chapter to a book.

⑥ **Variation**

Have students meet with the member(s) of other group(s) who has (have) the same information they do. Ask them to share ideas on their understanding of the material and how it might best be taught to their own group. Then go back and teach it to their group.

 PLEASE NOTE!

⑥ **The variations are endless.** The concept to keep in mind is to force interdependence.

THOUGHTS...

_____
_____
_____
_____
_____
_____

 INCLUSION  CONTROL  AFFECTION COMPETENCY

                                                          ✓✓

HELPING KIDS STAY ON TASK

WHAT'S THE POINT?

 To help kids stay on task. Once the assignment is given, actively monitoring the classroom can help kids get off to a good start and attend to the task at hand.

DESCRIPTION OF THE TECHNIQUE:

- **Give the assignment verbally and in written form on the board.**
- **Ask if there are any last minute questions.**
- **State what you will be doing and the procedure for asking for help.**
  - "I will be walking around the classroom. If you need help please raise your hand."
  - "I will be working with a small group in the corner, please do the best you can and save your questions for when I'm through with the group."
- **State the time limit for the assignment.**
  - "I will be collecting all papers at the end of the period."
  - "I will be changing the activity at 1:00."
- **State the expectations for what they can do if they finish early.** These should not be stated as rewards for early completion, but rather as opportunities for further learning.
- **Some ideas are:**
  - Research time on the computer (not game time).
  - Reading.
  - Extension activities that support the concept learned.
  - Volunteer to help students having difficulties.

PLEASE NOTE!

- **What works best in helping students stay on task is to be available as much as possible, constantly circulating the room and interacting with the students like you like them; not looking for misbehavior or mistakes.**

- **Sitting at your desk and glaring will not get the job done.**

THOUGHTS...

_____
_____
_____
_____
_____
_____
_____
_____
_____
_____

LETTING STUDENTS IN ON WHAT YOU ARE TEACHING

Sharing the Instructional Goals

WHAT'S THE POINT?

🌀 **To begin each day or each class by letting students know what the goal(s) for the lessons are.** This helps students focus on the task at hand and eliminates uncertainty and anxiety.

DESCRIPTION OF THE TECHNIQUE:

🌀 **Every day or each period inform students of:**
- Your goals for the lesson(s).
- An overview of what they will be learning.
- Any activity or work they will be expected to do.
- The time frame allotted.

🌀 **Variations**
- Do for each lesson or each period.
- Do for the week or for each unit of study.
- Do for the semester or the length of the class.
- The younger the kids the more immediate the goals need to be.

PLEASE NOTE!

🌀 To address various learning styles give verbally and write or have written on the board.
🌀 Be as precise as possible, so students come to see that your framing is accurate.
🌀 Do on a regular basis even if the goals and activities remain the same for days at a time.

THOUGHTS...

_____
_____
_____
_____
_____
_____
_____
_____
_____
_____

GRADING SO KIDS WILL LEARN

WHAT'S THE POINT?

◉ **To use letter grades in a manner that encourages mastery.** Students who regularly get low grades tend to become discouraged and give up on learning. On the other hand, saying no student can fail no matter what they produce quite frankly makes kids think we are crazy. The idea outlined below works where schools are focused on student mastery and are uncomfortable using anything other than letter grades.

DESCRIPTION OF THE TECHNIQUE:

◉ **Use a grading system that uses A's, B's, and Incompletes.**
- A student receiving anything lower than a B is given an Incomplete.
- The student is given a designated period of time to make up the work and/or retake the test until the B grade is achieved.
- The Incomplete is then removed and replaced with a B.
- If the work is not redone within the specified time, the D remains.
- The hope is that students who might settle for a C will not be as accepting of a D and will work to remove it.
- Students who use "redo's" are noted in the grade book to differentiate them from students who get A's and B's on the first try.

PLEASE NOTE!

◉ **This is not something a classroom teacher can do without support.** It is imperative that the concept be approved by the administrator in charge and thoroughly discussed with parents and students. It can, however, be used on less than a building-wide basis. In other words, one or two teachers can experiment with the idea for a specified period of time without affecting the whole school or having all classrooms involved.

THOUGHTS...

_____
_____
_____
_____
_____
_____
_____
_____
_____
_____
_____
_____
_____

HOW MUCH HOMEWORK IS ENOUGH?

WHAT'S THE POINT?

⑥ To assign the optimal amount of homework: enough to increase the learning but not so much as to discourage the learner.

DESCRIPTION OF THE TECHNIQUE:

⑥ **The age old question, how much homework to assign?**

- Research has shown that an hour or more of homework at the middle school/junior high and high school level can in most students increase learning. This much in elementary students, while perhaps initially increasing learning (as measured by test scores) often has a negative effect in the long run. There are several problems. First, the younger the student, the shorter the attention span. Thus for a first grader, after about 10 minutes, the law of diminishing returns sets in. Second, with 20 to 30 minutes or more per night with younger students, parents often have to get involved to see that the work is completed. This often sets up a negative interaction between parent and child around school work. Third, students burn out. By junior high they are sick of homework and when it really could be helpful, they rebel and begin to do little or none.

⑥ **So what to do?**

- **Elementary School:** Ten minutes total per night Monday through Thursday per grade level is shown by research to be optimal. Thus 10 minutes for first grade and 40 or so for fourth.

- **Middle School/Junior High:** Continuing the 10 minute per grade level guideline, one to one and a half hours total per night Monday through Friday seems to be optimal.

- **High School:** Depending on the nature of the community and the students attending, one to three hours total per night Monday through Friday can produce higher achievement scores.

PLEASE NOTE!

⑥ **It is not just the number of minutes spent on homework, but also the quality of the work assigned that is important.** Homework for the sake of homework is often meaningless busy work. These time guidelines are for the amount of time it takes the student to complete the work, not the amount of work assigned. In other words, a student with learning problems will not accomplish as much as some other students in the same amount of time. Thus some modification of homework assignments will be needed.

continued on next page

These guidelines are just that, general guidelines. You will never go wrong by using plain old common sense when assigning homework. A long term paper due the same Friday as Homecoming is probably not the greatest idea.

THOUGHTS...

HOMEWORK - COLLECTING IT
The KIST Approach

WHAT'S THE POINT?

⑥ **To handle the collection of homework in a manner that keeps the problem of doing or not doing the homework in the hands of the person who owns it - the student.** In other words **KIST** (**K**eep **I**t **S**imple **T**eacher).

DESCRIPTION OF THE TECHNIQUE:

⑥ **Get the class started with something that has to do with academic learning** (see **STARTING THE CLASS**).
⑥ **Walk around the room, approaching students one at a time.**
⑥ **Using the student's name say "homework please."**
⑥ **If the student hands you the homework say "Thanks."**
⑥ **If the student doesn't have the homework say "How sad," or if you can't get the words out, at least look sad and concerned and move on.**
⑥ **When you've asked every student, put the homework on your desk and continue teaching.**

⑥ **Variations**
   • Some teachers take roll as they collect the homework.
   • Some teachers have students trade papers and correct, and then collect.
   • Some teachers have students self-correct as they go over the work with the students and then collect.

PLEASE NOTE!

⑥ **The point is to personally ask each student daily for their homework, and drop the rewards or punishments.** As one teacher said, "I don't have to stay after school and look at them for thirty minutes. I don't have to spend my money on stars and goodies. I just walk around and say 'Thanks, thanks. How sad, how sad'." Most teachers report an increase in the amount of homework coming in after two to three months of this approach.

 INCLUSION  CONTROL AFFECTION COMPETENCY

GRADING PAPERS IN A POSITIVE WAY
Nix the Red Ink and The Number Wrong

 WHAT'S THE POINT?

⊚ **To provide students with feedback on their work that emphasizes that it is OK to make mistakes, and that we learn from our mistakes.**

 DESCRIPTION OF THE TECHNIQUE:

⊚ **Here are some ideas that other teachers have found helpful:**
- Nix the red ink. Use any color but red. In our society red on a paper means bad, bad, bad.
- Nix the X's and the O's. These say bad, bad, bad. Try using a slash, a question mark or a note "Please correct."
- Put big C's on everything that is correct, leaving the incorrect answers unmarked.
- Indicate the number correct (+ 21) rather than the number wrong (-10).
- Write comments like "Help me understand this." "How could you make this clearer?" "What could you do to develop this point further?" etc.

 PLEASE NOTE!

⊚ **Mistakes do need to be pointed out and corrected.** It's how we do it that determines whether the kid feels shame, blame, and stupid or is encouraged to correct and grow.

THOUGHTS...

_____
_____
_____
_____
_____
_____
_____
_____
_____
_____
_____
_____
_____
_____
_____
_____
_____
_____
_____

 INCLUSION  CONTROL  AFFECTION COMPETENCY

✔

✔✔

GETTING STUDENTS TO RECOGNIZE THEIR STRENGTHS
Attribution Theory

WHAT'S THE POINT?

⑥ **To get students to recognize and verbalize their strengths including the reasons behind any improvement.** While to adults the fact that studying harder often leads to better grades and that everyone has areas of strength, this is often not as apparent to some students, especially those not doing well in school.

DESCRIPTION OF THE TECHNIQUE:

⑥ **Adult Persuasion Statements**
- Let's start with what not to do because this is a technique that seems to roll off most of our lips. Understanding this will make what to do more understandable. In persuasion, the adult tries to persuade or convince the student that he should do something as in work harder.
  - "You should be studying more."
  - "If only you would pay more attention in class."
  - "I'm telling you that if you would spend more time practicing you would get better."
- These are basically you messages (see **I NEED AND I WILL**). The message is that the teacher is smarter than the student, the student doesn't want to be told what to do, he goes on the defensive and usually ends up doing the exact opposite of what the adult has told him to do.

⑥ **Adult Attribution Statements**
- These statements are one step up from persuasion; a little better but not the best. Here the adult states a positive attribute about the student.
  - "You sure are a good worker."
  - "You really know how to be a great friend."
  - "A strength of yours is math."
- The problem with these statements is that if the student has low self esteem or does not trust the teacher, he/she doesn't believe it. In fact, the student thinks the teacher is trying to manipulate her or as the kids say, "She's messing with my head."

⑥ **Student Attribution Statements**
- Now we have arrived at something that may produce behavior change in the student. By asking questions, we get the student to tell us what his strengths are or why she has scored better on the test. When the answer comes out of the student, the student is more apt to believe it.
  - "Tell me how you scored higher on that test?"

continued on next page

✓   ✓✓

- Some students need a little prod to come up with a reason. You might ask, "Did you study hard last night or are you just a good guesser."
- A more general question to ask would be:
  - "What is it that you do really well?"
- Again some students may need a little prodding as in, "Do you do better in spelling or in math?" or "Do you play baseball well or draw well?"

⑥ **Variation**

Student Attribution Statements also work well to help students understand why they did not do well. "How did you manage to only get two out of 20 right on your spelling test? Did you forget to study or are you just a poor guesser?"

⑥ Remember, drop the sarcasm. This is serious business.

 PLEASE NOTE!

⑥ **Give this one a try.** To a rational adult it does seem pretty lame, but used with a student who is struggling, it can work wonders.

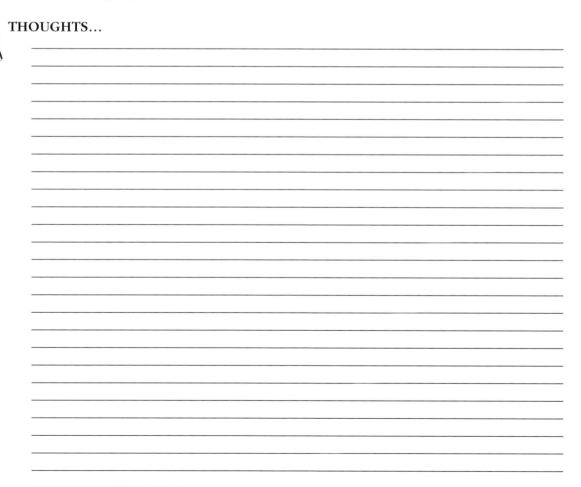 **THOUGHTS…**

DEALING WITH FAILURE

WHAT'S THE POINT?

⑥ **To identify and remediate the reason(s) behind a student's failure.** The focus is on the student and helping him or her discover what is causing the failure and then commit to a plan for change. Students generally fail in school for one of the following reasons:
- They can't do the work assigned.
- The work is inappropriate or too hard.
- They think they can't do the work assigned.
- Low self esteem or years of failure.
- They are in power struggles, usually with one or both of their parents and sometimes with the school.
- They really just don't care anymore.
- Too little parent and community modeling.
- Too many years of failure.

DESCRIPTION OF THE TECHNIQUE:

⑥ **The way to get kids to start succeeding is to first get them to identify why they are failing and then to make a commitment to a plan for change.**

⑥ **Some ways to accomplish this are:**
- Ask "what" and "why" questions. "What would you like to see change?" "What do you think you need to help you succeed next time?"
- Use the "Help me understand" statement. "Help me understand what you're trying to tell me when you act like the class clown every period."
- When students say they don't know why they're failing use the "Some students aren't doing well because they don't understand. Some students don't do the work because it makes their parents mad. Could any of these be you?" technique.

⑥ **The point is to get the student to tell you, not you tell the student.**

⑥ **Once the student has identified why he is failing, help him make a plan.** Some options to have the students consider are:
- Offering some of your time to help them privately.
- Suggesting tutoring or additional outside help.
- Offering testing to see if they have special needs.
- Asking them how the curriculum could be modified to better meet their needs.
- Offering some help in organizational and study skills.
- Just saying frankly, "You're in the ninth grade reading at a third grade level. Do you want to do something about it? Or do you just want to keep acting like the class clown to avoid facing the problem?"

continued on next page

 INCLUSION  CONTROL  AFFECTION COMPETENCY

✔

✔✔

 PLEASE NOTE!

⑥ **The point to keep in mind is that the student must identify the source of the problem and make a commitment to the change before you're going to see any real improvement.** It's also important to take a look at your own ideas and beliefs about the student. Are you sending the wrong message? Make sure the student knows that you don't consider him or her dumb. Refrain from lecturing or moralizing and don't get sucked into rewards and punishment. They don't work, especially after the first few years of school. And finally, acknowledge each small step toward improvement.

THOUGHTS...

 INCLUSION  CONTROL  AFFECTION COMPETENCY

✓   ✓✓

TAKING ATTENDANCE
Who's job is it?

 WHAT'S THE POINT?

⑥ **To teach students from kindergarten through high school to take attendance.** This frees the teacher from a repetitious and tedious job, lets students assume more responsibility, and helps kids get to know other students' names.

 DESCRIPTION OF THE TECHNIQUE:

⑥ **Younger students:**
 • Have a chart with a pocket space for each student.
 • Label each pocket with a student name.
 • Have each student draw themselves or use a photograph and glue it to a popcicle stick. You can also use 3" X 5" cards.
 • Hold students responsible for putting their "face on a stick" or card in their name pocket each morning.
 • Have a student remove the sticks/cards at the end of the day.

⑥ **Older students:**
 • Assign a student to take attendance on a weekly attendance sheet.
 • Check for accuracy as you feel the need. You post in your attendance book at the end of each week.

⑥ **An academic approach:**
 • Make a lesson out of taking attendance by adding and subtracting those present and those absent, etc.

THOUGHTS...

_____
_____
_____
_____
_____
_____
_____
_____
_____
_____
_____
_____
_____

BIBLIOGRAPHY:

Audio Tapes - Betsy Geddes, Ed.D., Geddes Consulting, P.O. Box 82759, Portland, OR 97282.
- Creating Consistent School Discipline
- Handling Misbehavior In The Classroom
- Preventing Misbehavior In The Classroom
- Responsible Parents Raise Responsible Kids

Call 1-800-392-5204 to order.

Cline/Fay Love and Logic Institute, Inc., books, tapes & videos, 2207 Jackson St., Golden, CO 80401.
Call 1-800-338-4065 for a free catalog.

All About Attention Deficit Disorder, Thomas W. Phelan, PhD., Child Management, Inc., 1993.

Beyond Discipline, Alfie Kohn, ASCD, 1996.

Building Self-Concept in Children, Patricia Berne, Continuum Press, 1981.

Control Theory in the Classroom, W. Glasser, Perennial Library, 1986.

Dealing With People You Can't Stand, Dr. Rick Brinkman and Dr. Rick Kirschner, McGraw-Hill, Inc., 1994.

The Death of Common Sense, Philip K. Howard, Random House, 1994.

Emotional Intelligence, David Goleman, Bantam Books, 1995.

The Emotional Problems of Normal Children, Stanley Turechi, M.D., Bantam Books, 1994.

First Things First, Stephen R. Covey, A. Roger Merrill, Rebecca R. Merrill, Simon & Schuster, 1994.

For Your Own Good, Alice Miller, The Noonday Press, 1883.

High Risk: Children Without a Conscience, Ken Magid and Carol McKelvey, M & M Publishing, 1987.

I Am Not A Short Adult, Marilyn Burns, Little, Brown, 1977.

Life in a Crowded Place: Making a Learning Community, Ralph Peterson, Heinemann, 1992.

On Raising Kids, Sylvia Rimm, Apple Publishing Company, 1992.

Parenting With Love and Logic, Foster Cline and Jim Fay, Pinon Press, 1990.

Parenting So Kids Can Learn, Sylvia Rimm, Ph. D., Educational Assessment Service, Inc.

Parenting Teens With Love and Logic, Foster Cline and Jim Fay, Pinon Press, 1992.

Punished by Rewards, Alfie Kohn, Houghton Mifflin Co., 1993.

Raising Self-Reliant Children in a Self-Indulgent World, Stephen H. Glen and Jane Nelson, St. Martins Press, 1992.

Schools Without Failure, W. Glasser, Harper & Row, 1969.

Seven Habits of Highly Effective People, Stephen R. Covey, Simon & Schuster, Inc., 1989.

Special Education Law, L.F. Rothstein, Longman, 1990.

The Quality School Teacher, W. Glasser, Harper-Perennial, 1993.

Teaching With Love and Logic, Jim Fay and David Funk, Love and Logic Press, Inc., 1995.

Underachievement Syndrome: Causes and Cures, Sylvia Rimm, PhD., Educational Assessment Service, Inc., 1987.

Why We Do What We Do, Edward L. Deci, Penguin Books, 1996.

ORDER FORM

800-338-4065

PLEASE SEND THE ITEM(S) BELOW TO:

Name _____ Phone (___) _____

Address _____

City _____ State _____ Zip _____

TO ORDER THE BOOK:

Students Speak:
Effect Discipline For Today's Students   **$24.95**   Quantity _____ $ _____
A book that helps us understand what students need and want in
school. A book packed with Winning Ways, ideas for immediate
classroom use that will improve student behavior and increase
student achievement. A BOOK BY TEACHERS FOR TEACHERS.

TO ORDER SUPPORTIVE TAPES:

Creating Consistent School Discipline   **$13.95**   Quantity _____ $ _____
A single audio tape covering the three basic approaches to school
discipline. If your school is looking for consistency, this is the tape.

Preventing Misbehavior in Your Classroom   **$21.95**   Quantity _____ $ _____
Want to head off misbehavior? Here is a two tape audio set with
14 tried and true ways to head off misbehavior in your classroom.

Handling Misbehavior In Your Classroom   **$21.95**   Quantity _____ $ _____
What do we do and say when the student does and says? This two tape audio
 set presents 12 intervention techniques that are practical and "do-able."

Responsible Parents Raise Responsible Kids   **$21.95**   Quantity _____ $ _____
This two tape audio set will help you discover your parenting style
and give you techniques for turning your kids into responsible
human beings.

SUBTOTAL $ _____

SHIPPING & HANDLING:

Orders of $35.00 or less.........$5.50   Orders of $75.01–100.........$11.00
Orders of $35.01–50..............$7.00   Orders of $100.01–150........$14.00 $ _____
Orders of $50.01–75..............$9.00   Orders of $150.01–200........$18.00
                                              Orders over $200...................10%

(Maximum of $40.00)
For APO, Hawaii, Alaska, Canada and foreign orders, please call for shipping/handling charges, 1-800-338-4065   **TOTAL $ _____**

PAYMENT ENCLOSED — Payable to **Love and Logic Institute, Inc.**
☐ CHECK   ☐ CREDIT CARD   ☐ MONEY ORDER   ☐ SCHOOL PURCHASE ORDER
             ___ VISA   (Please attach a copy with your order)
             ___ MASTERCARD
             ___ DISCOVER

MAIL TO: LOVE AND LOGIC INSTITUTE, INC., 2207 JACKSON ST., GOLDEN, CO 80401 OR CALL 800-338-4065 OR VISIT www.loveandlogic.com